THIS BOOK IS THE PROPERTY OF

NAME ______________________________

ADDRESS ______________________________

CITY ____________________ STATE ____________

NAME OF CHURCH ______________________________

GROWING IN CHRIST

GROWING IN CHRIST

An Exposition of Luther's Small Catechism

Illustrated by George Kuhasz and Harry Tillson

CONCORDIA PUBLISHING HOUSE
SAINT LOUIS, MISSOURI

CONCORDIA PUBLISHING HOUSE
St. Louis, Missouri

PRINTED IN U.S.A.

GROWING IN CHRIST

An Exposition of Luther's Small Catechism

Illustrated by George Kuhasz and Harry Tillson

CONCORDIA PUBLISHING HOUSE
SAINT LOUIS, MISSOURI

CONCORDIA PUBLISHING HOUSE
St. Louis, Missouri

PRINTED IN U. S. A.

CONTENTS

CONTENTS

In the year 1529 Dr. Martin Luther wrote his Small Catechism for the instruction of children

PART ONE

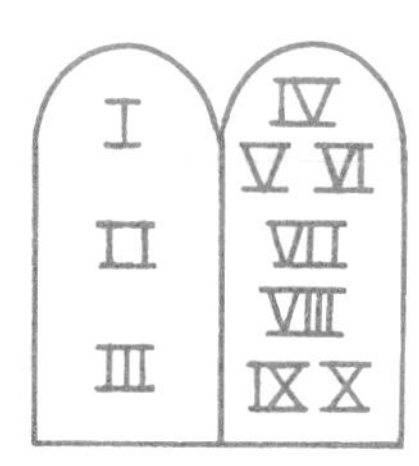

SECTION ONE

The Ten Commandments

AS THE HEAD OF THE FAMILY SHOULD TEACH THEM IN A SIMPLE WAY TO HIS HOUSEHOLD

THE FIRST COMMANDMENT

Thou shalt have no other gods before Me.

What does this mean?

We should fear, love, and trust in God above all things.

THE SECOND COMMANDMENT

Thou shalt not take the name of the Lord, thy God, in vain.

What does this mean?

**We should fear and love God that we may
not curse, swear, use witchcraft, lie, or deceive by His name,
but call upon it in every trouble,
pray, praise, and give thanks.**

THE THIRD COMMANDMENT

Remember the Sabbath day, to keep it holy.

What does this mean?

**We should fear and love God that we may
not despise preaching and His Word,
but hold it sacred and gladly hear and learn it.**

THE FOURTH COMMANDMENT

**Thou shalt honor thy father and thy mother,
that it may be well with thee,
and thou mayest live long on the earth.**

What does this mean?

We should fear and love God that we may
not despise our parents and masters, nor provoke them to anger,
but give them honor, serve and obey them,
and hold them in love and esteem.

THE FIFTH COMMANDMENT

Thou shalt not kill.

What does this mean?

We should fear and love God that we may
not hurt nor harm our neighbor in his body,
but help and befriend him in every bodily need.

THE SIXTH COMMANDMENT

Thou shalt not commit adultery.

What does this mean?

We should fear and love God that we may
lead a chaste and decent life in word and deed,
and each love and honor his spouse.

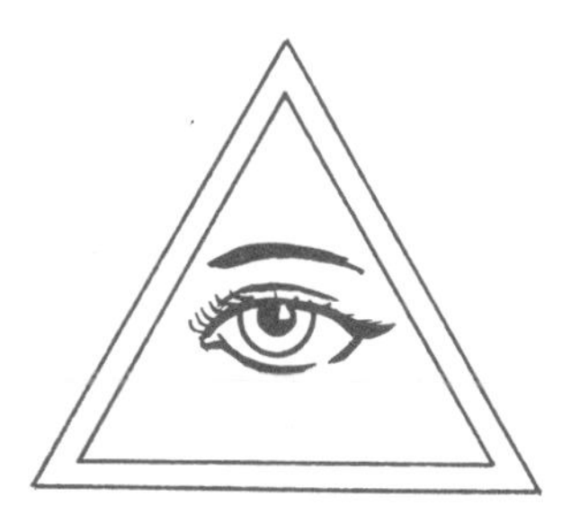

THE SEVENTH COMMANDMENT

Thou shalt not steal.

What does this mean?

We should fear and love God that we may
not take our neighbor's money or goods,
nor get them by false ware or dealing,
but help him to improve and protect his property and business.

THE EIGHTH COMMANDMENT

Thou shalt not bear false witness against thy neighbor.

What does this mean?

We should fear and love God that we may
not deceitfully belie, betray, slander, nor defame our neighbor,
but defend him, speak well of him, and put the best construction on everything.

THE NINTH COMMANDMENT

Thou shalt not covet thy neighbor's house.

What does this mean?

We should fear and love God that we may
not craftily seek to get our neighbor's inheritance or house,
nor obtain it by a show of right,
but help and be of service to him in keeping it.

THE TENTH COMMANDMENT

**Thou shalt not covet thy neighbor's wife,
nor his manservant, nor his maidservant,
nor his cattle,
nor anything that is thy neighbor's.**

What does this mean?

We should fear and love God that we may not
estrange, force, or entice away from our neighbor
his wife, servants, or cattle,
but urge them to stay and do their duty.

THE CLOSE OF THE COMMANDMENTS

What does God say of all these Commandments?

He says thus: I, the Lord, thy God, am a jealous God,
visiting the iniquity of the fathers upon the children
unto the third and fourth generation of them that hate Me,
and showing mercy unto thousands of them that love Me
and keep My Commandments.

What does this mean?

God threatens to punish all that transgress these
Commandments.
Therefore we should fear His wrath and not act contrary
to them.
But He promises grace and every blessing to all that keep
these Commandments.
Therefore we should also love and trust in Him
and willingly do according to His Commandments.

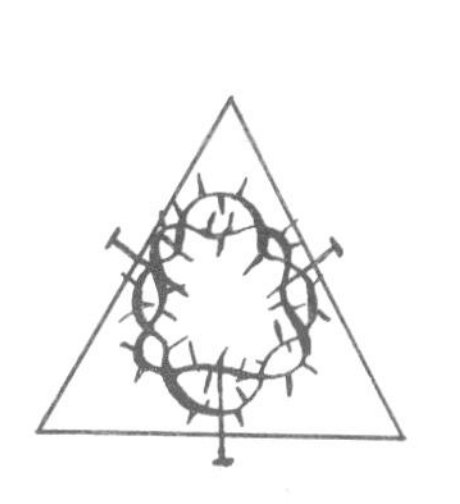

The Apostles' Creed

AS THE HEAD OF THE FAMILY SHOULD TEACH IT IN A SIMPLE WAY TO HIS HOUSEHOLD

THE FIRST ARTICLE — *Creation*

I believe in God the Father Almighty,
Maker of heaven and earth.

What does this mean?

I believe that God has made me and all creatures;
that He has given me my body and soul, eyes, ears, and all my members,
my reason and all my senses, and still preserves them;
also clothing and shoes, meat and drink, house and home,
wife and children, fields, cattle, and all my goods;
that He richly and daily provides me with all that I need
to support this body and life;
that He defends me against all danger,
and guards and protects me from all evil;
and all this purely out of fatherly, divine goodness and mercy,
without any merit or worthiness in me;
for all which it is my duty to thank and praise, to serve and obey Him.
This is most certainly true.

THE SECOND ARTICLE — *Redemption*

And [I believe] in Jesus Christ, His only Son, our Lord,
who was conceived by the Holy Ghost,
born of the Virgin Mary,
suffered under Pontius Pilate,
was crucified, dead, and buried;
He descended into hell;
the third day He rose again from the dead;
He ascended into heaven,
and sitteth on the right hand of God the Father Almighty;
from thence He shall come to judge the quick and the dead.

What does this mean?

I believe that Jesus Christ,
true God, begotten of the Father from eternity, and also true man, born of the Virgin Mary,
is my Lord,
who has redeemed me, a lost and condemned creature,
purchased and won me from all sins, from death, and from the power of the devil;
not with gold or silver, but with His holy, precious blood and with His innocent suffering and death,
that I may be His own, and live under Him in His kingdom, and serve Him in everlasting righteousness, innocence, and blessedness,
even as He is risen from the dead, lives and reigns to all eternity.
This is most certainly true.

THE THIRD ARTICLE — *Sanctification*

I believe in the Holy Ghost;
the holy Christian Church, the communion of saints;
the forgiveness of sins;
the resurrection of the body;
and the life everlasting. Amen.

What does this mean?

I believe that I cannot by my own reason or strength
believe in Jesus Christ, my Lord, or come to Him;
but the Holy Ghost has called me by the Gospel,
enlightened me with His gifts,
sanctified and kept me in the true faith;
even as He calls, gathers, enlightens, and sanctifies
the whole Christian Church on earth, and keeps it
with Jesus Christ in the one true faith;
in which Christian Church He daily and richly forgives all
sins to me and all believers,
and will at the Last Day raise up me and all the dead,
and give unto me and all believers in Christ eternal life.
This is most certainly true.

The Lord's Prayer

AS THE HEAD OF THE FAMILY SHOULD TEACH IT IN A SIMPLE WAY TO HIS HOUSEHOLD

Our Father who art in heaven.
Hallowed be Thy name.
Thy kingdom come.
Thy will be done on earth as it is in heaven.
Give us this day our daily bread.
And forgive us our trespasses,
as we forgive those who trespass against us.
And lead us not into temptation,
but deliver us from evil.
For Thine is the kingdom
and the power and the glory forever and ever.
Amen.

THE INTRODUCTION

Our Father who art in heaven.

What does this mean?

God would by these words tenderly invite us to believe that He is our true Father, and that we are His true children, so that we may with all boldness and confidence ask Him as dear children ask their dear father.

THE FIRST PETITION

Hallowed be Thy name.

What does this mean?

God's name is indeed holy in itself;
but we pray in this petition
that it may be holy among us also.

How is this done?

When the Word of God is taught in its truth and purity,
and we, as the children of God,
also lead a holy life according to it.
This grant us, dear Father in heaven.
But he that teaches and lives otherwise than God's Word teaches,
profanes the name of God among us.
From this preserve us, Heavenly Father.

THE SECOND PETITION

Thy kingdom come.

What does this mean?

The kingdom of God comes indeed without our prayer, of itself;
but we pray in this petition
that it may come unto us also.

How is this done?

When our heavenly Father gives us His Holy Spirit,
so that by His grace we believe His holy Word and
lead a godly life, here in time and hereafter in eternity

THE THIRD PETITION

Thy will be done on earth as it is in heaven.

What does this mean?

The good and gracious will of God is done indeed without our prayer;
but we pray in this petition
that it may be done among us also.

How is this done?

When God breaks and hinders every evil counsel and will
which would not let us hallow God's name
nor let His kingdom come,
such as the will of the devil, the world, and our flesh;
but strengthens and preserves us steadfast
in His Word and faith unto our end.
This is His gracious and good will.

THE FOURTH PETITION

Give us this day our daily bread.

What does this mean?

God gives daily bread indeed without our prayer,
also to all the wicked;
but we pray in this petition
that He would lead us to know it, and to receive
our daily bread with thanksgiving.

What is meant by daily bread?

Everything that belongs to the support and wants of the body,
such as food, drink, clothing, shoes,
house, home, field, cattle, money,, goods,
a pious spouse, pious children, pious servants,
pious and faithful rulers, good government,
good weather, peace, health, discipline, honor,
good friends, faithful neighbors, and the like.

THE FIFTH PETITION

And forgive us our trespasses, as we forgive those who trespass against us.

What does this mean?

We pray in this petition
that our Father in heaven would not look upon our sins,
nor on their account deny our prayer;
for we are worthy of none of the things for which we pray,
neither have we deserved them;
but that He would grant them all to us by grace;
for we daily sin much and indeed deserve nothing
but punishment.
So will we also heartily forgive, and readily do good to,
those who sin against us.

THE SIXTH PETITION

And lead us not into temptation.

What does this mean?

God indeed tempts no one;
but we pray in this petition that God would guard
and keep us,
so that the devil, the world, and our flesh may not deceive us
nor seduce us into misbelief, despair, and other great shame
and vice;
and though we be assailed by them,
that still we may finally overcome and obtain the victory.

THE SEVENTH PETITION

But deliver us from evil.

What does this mean?

We pray in this petition, as the sum of all,
that our Father in heaven would deliver us from every evil of body and soul, property and honor,
and finally, when our last hour has come, grant us a blessed end,
and graciously take us from this vale of tears to Himself in heaven.

THE CONCLUSION

For Thine is the kingdom and the power and the glory forever and ever. Amen.

What is meant by the word "Amen"?

That I should be certain that these petitions
are acceptable to our Father in heaven, and are heard by Him;
for He Himself has commanded us so to pray,
and has promised to hear us.
Amen, Amen, that is, Yea, yea, it shall be so.

The Sacrament of Holy Baptism

AS THE HEAD OF THE FAMILY SHOULD TEACH IT IN A SIMPLE WAY TO HIS HOUSEHOLD

I. THE NATURE OF BAPTISM

What is Baptism?

Baptism is not simple water only, but it is the water comprehended in God's command and connected with God's word.

Which is that word of God?

Christ, our Lord, says in the last chapter of Matthew: Go ye and teach all nations, baptizing them in the name of the Father and of the Son and of the Holy Ghost.

II. THE BLESSINGS OF BAPTISM

What does Baptism give or profit?

**It works forgiveness of sins,
delivers from death and the devil, and
gives eternal salvation to all who believe this,
as the words and promises of God declare.**

Which are such words and promises of God?

Christ, our Lord, says in the last chapter of Mark: He that believeth and is baptized shall be saved; but he that believeth not shall be damned.

III. THE POWER OF BAPTISM

How can water do such great things?

It is not the water indeed that does them, but the word of God which is in and with the water, and faith, which trusts such word of God in the water.
For without the word of God the water is simple water and no Baptism.
But with the word of God it is a Baptism, that is,
a gracious water of life and a washing of regeneration in the Holy Ghost, as St. Paul says, Titus, chapter third:
[According to His mercy He saved us] By the washing of regeneration
and renewing of the Holy Ghost,
which He shed on us abundantly through Jesus Christ, our Savior,
that, being justified by His grace,
we should be made heirs according to the hope of eternal life.
This is a faithful saying.

IV. THE SIGNIFICANCE OF BAPTIZING WITH WATER

What does such baptizing with water signify?

It signifies that the Old Adam in us should,
by daily contrition and repentance,
be drowned and die with all sins and evil lusts
and, again, a new man daily come forth and arise,
who shall live before God in righteousness and purity forever.

Where is this written?

St. Paul writes, Romans, chapter sixth:
We are buried with Christ by Baptism into death,
that,
like as He was raised up from the dead by the glory of the Father,
even so we also should walk in newness of life.

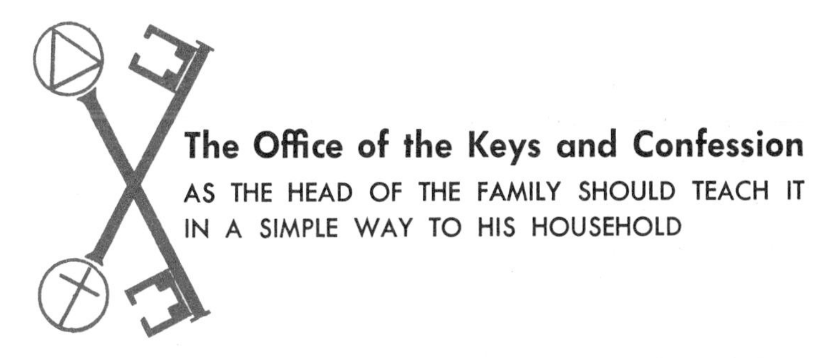

The Office of the Keys and Confession

AS THE HEAD OF THE FAMILY SHOULD TEACH IT
IN A SIMPLE WAY TO HIS HOUSEHOLD

What is the Office of the Keys?

**It is the peculiar church power
which Christ has given to His Church on earth
to forgive the sins of penitent sinners, but
to retain the sins of the impenitent
as long as they do not repent.**

Where is this written?

**Thus writes the holy Evangelist John, chapter twentieth:
The Lord Jesus breathed on His disciples and saith
unto them,
Receive ye the Holy Ghost.
Whosesoever sins ye remit, they are remitted unto them; and
whosesoever sins ye retain, they are retained.**

What do you believe according to these words?

**I believe that,
when the called ministers of Christ deal with us
by His divine command,
especially when they exclude manifest and impenitent
sinners
from the Christian congregation,
and, again,
when they absolve those who repent of their sins
and are willing to amend,
this is as valid and certain, in heaven also,
as if Christ, our dear Lord, dealt with us Himself.**

What is Confession?

Confession embraces two parts.
One is that we confess our sins;
the other, that we receive absolution, or forgiveness,
from the pastor
as from God Himself,
and in no wise doubt, but firmly believe,
that by it our sins are forgiven
before God in heaven.

What sins should we confess?

Before God we should plead guilty of all sins,
even of those which we do not know,
as we do in the Lord's Prayer;
but before the pastor we should confess those sins only
which we know and feel in our hearts.

Which are these?

Here consider your station according to the
Ten Commandments,
whether you are a father, mother, son, daughter, master,
mistress, servant;
whether you have been disobedient, unfaithful, slothful;
whether you have grieved any person by word or deed;
whether you have stolen, neglected, or wasted aught,
or done other injury.

The Sacrament of the Altar

AS THE HEAD OF THE FAMILY SHOULD TEACH IT IN A SIMPLE WAY TO HIS HOUSEHOLD

What is the Sacrament of the Altar?

It is the true body and blood of our Lord Jesus Christ
under the bread and wine,
for us Christians to eat and to drink,
instituted by Christ Himself.

Where is this written?

The holy Evangelists Matthew, Mark, Luke, and St. Paul [the Apostle] write thus:
Our Lord Jesus Christ, the same night in which He was betrayed, took bread; and when He had given thanks, He brake it and gave it to His disciples, saying,
Take, eat; this is My body, which is given for you.
This do in remembrance of Me.
After the same manner also He took the cup when He had supped, and
when He had given thanks, He gave it to them, saying,
Drink ye all of it;
this cup is the new testament in My blood, which is shed for you for the remission of sins.
This do, as oft as ye drink it, in remembrance of Me.

What is the benefit of such eating and drinking?

That is shown us by these words,
"Given and shed for you for the remission of sins";
namely, that in the Sacrament
forgiveness of sins, life, and salvation are given us through these words.
For where there is forgiveness of sins, there is also life and salvation.

How can bodily eating and drinking do such great things?

It is not the eating and drinking indeed that does them,
but the words here written,
"Given and shed for you for the remission of sins";
which words, besides the bodily eating and drinking,
are the chief thing in the Sacrament;
and he that believes these words has what they say and express,
namely, the forgiveness of sins.

Who, then, receives such Sacrament worthily?

Fasting and bodily preparation are indeed a fine outward training; but
he is truly worthy and well prepared who has faith in these words,
"Given and shed for you for the remission of sins."
But he that does not believe these words, or doubts,
is unworthy and unprepared;
for the words "for you" require all hearts to believe.

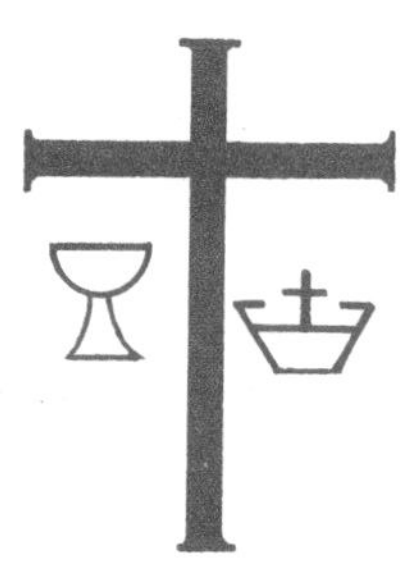

SECTION TWO

Daily Prayers

HOW THE HEAD OF THE FAMILY SHOULD TEACH HIS HOUSEHOLD TO PRAY MORNING AND EVENING

MORNING PRAYER

In the morning, when you get up, make the sign of the holy cross and say:

In the name of ✠ the Father and of the Son and of the Holy Ghost. Amen.

Then, kneeling or standing, repeat the Creed and the Lord's Prayer. If you choose, you may also say this little prayer:

I thank Thee, my heavenly Father,
through Jesus Christ, Thy dear Son,
that Thou hast kept me this night from all harm and danger;
and I pray Thee that Thou wouldst keep me this day also from sin and every evil,
that all my doings and life may please Thee.
For into Thy hands I commend myself,
my body and soul, and all things.
Let Thy holy angel be with me,
that the wicked Foe may have no power over me. Amen.

Then go joyfully to your work, singing a hymn, like that of the Ten Commandments, or whatever your devotion may suggest.

EVENING PRAYER

In the evening, when you go to bed, make the sign of the holy cross and say:

In the name of ✠ the Father and of the Son and of the Holy Ghost. Amen.

Then, kneeling or standing, repeat the Creed and the Lord's Prayer. If you choose, you may also say this little prayer:

**I thank Thee, my heavenly Father,
through Jesus Christ, Thy dear Son,
that Thou hast graciously kept me this day;
and I pray Thee that Thou wouldst forgive me all my sins where I have done wrong,
and graciously keep me this night.
For into Thy hands I commend myself,
my body and soul, and all things.
Let Thy holy angel be with me,
that the wicked Foe may have no power over me. Amen.**

Then go to sleep at once and in good cheer.

HOW THE HEAD OF THE FAMILY SHOULD TEACH HIS HOUSEHOLD TO ASK A BLESSING AND RETURN THANKS

ASKING A BLESSING

The children and members of the household shall go to the table reverently, fold their hands, and say:

The eyes of all wait upon Thee, O Lord,
and Thou givest them their meat in due season;
Thou openest Thine hand and satisfiest the desire of every living thing.

Then shall be said the Lord's Prayer and the following:

Lord God, Heavenly Father, bless us and these Thy gifts
which we receive from Thy bountiful goodness,
through Jesus Christ, our Lord. Amen.

RETURNING THANKS

Also, after eating, they shall, in like manner, reverently and with folded hands say:

Oh, give thanks unto the Lord,
for He is good, for His mercy endureth forever.
He giveth food to all flesh;
He giveth to the beast his food,
and to the young ravens which cry.
He delighteth not in the strength of the horse.
He taketh not pleasure in the legs of a man.
The Lord taketh pleasure in them that fear Him,
in those that hope in His mercy.

Then shall be said the Lord's Prayer and the following:

We thank Thee, Lord God, Heavenly Father, through Jesus Christ, our Lord, for all Thy benefits, who livest and reignest forever and ever. Amen.

SECTION THREE

Table of Duties

OR CERTAIN PASSAGES OF SCRIPTURE FOR VARIOUS HOLY ORDERS AND ESTATES WHEREBY THESE ARE SEVERALLY TO BE ADMONISHED AS TO THEIR OFFICE AND DUTY

TO BISHOPS, PASTORS, AND PREACHERS

A bishop must be blameless, the husband of one wife, vigilant, sober, of good behavior, given to hospitality, apt to teach; not given to wine, no striker, not greedy of filthy lucre; but patient, not a brawler, not covetous; one that ruleth well his own house, having his children in subjection with all gravity; not a novice; holding fast the faithful Word as he hath been taught, that he may be able by sound doctrine both to exhort and to convince the gainsayers. ***1 Tim. 3:2, 3, 4, 6; Titus 1:9.***

WHAT THE HEARERS OWE TO THEIR PASTORS

Eat and drink such things as they give; for the laborer is worthy of his hire. ***Luke 10:7.***

Even so hath the Lord ordained that they which preach the Gospel should live of the Gospel. *1 Cor. 9:14.*

Let him that is taught in the Word communicate unto him that teacheth in all good things. Be not deceived; God is not mocked; for whatsoever a man soweth, that shall he also reap. *Gal. 6:6, 7.*

Let the elders that rule well be counted worthy of double honor, especially they who labor in the Word and doctrine. For the Scripture saith, Thou shalt not muzzle the ox that treadeth out the corn; and, The laborer is worthy of his reward. *1 Tim. 5:17, 18.*

And we beseech you, brethren, to know them which labor among you and are over you in the Lord and admonish you; and to esteem them very highly in love for their work's sake. And be at peace among yourselves. *1 Thess. 5:12, 13.*

Obey them that have the rule over you, and submit yourselves; for they watch for your souls as they that must give account, that they may do it with joy and not with grief, for that is unprofitable for you. *Heb. 13:17.*

OF CIVIL GOVERNMENT

Let every soul be subject unto the higher powers. For there is no power but of God; the powers that be are ordained of God. Whosoever therefore resisteth the power, resisteth the ordinance of God; and they that resist shall receive to themselves damnation. For rulers are not a terror to good works, but to the evil. Wilt thou, then, not be afraid of the power? Do that which is good, and thou shalt have praise of the same; for he is the minister of God to thee for good. But if thou do that which is evil, be afraid, for he beareth not the sword in vain; for he is the minister of God, a revenger to execute wrath upon him that doeth evil. *Rom. 13:1-4.*

OF SUBJECTS

Render unto Caesar the things which are Caesar's, and unto God the things that are God's. *Matt. 22:21.*

Wherefore ye must needs be subject, not only for wrath, but also for conscience' sake. For, for this cause pay ye tribute also; for they are God's ministers, attending continually upon this very thing. Render therefore to all their dues: tribute to whom tribute is due; custom, to whom custom; fear, to whom fear; honor, to whom honor. *Rom. 13:5-7.*

I exhort therefore that, first of all, supplications, prayers, intercessions, and giving of thanks be made for all men, for kings, and for all that are in authority, that we may lead a quiet and peaceable life in all godliness and honesty. For this is good and acceptable in the sight of God, our Savior. *1 Tim. 2:1-3.*

Put them in mind to be subject to principalities and powers, to obey magistrates, to be ready to every good work. *Titus 3:1.*

Submit yourselves to every ordinance of man for the Lord's sake: whether it be to the king, as supreme; or unto governors, as unto them that are sent by him for the punishment of evildoers, and for the praise of them that do well. *1 Peter 2:13, 14.*

TO HUSBANDS

Likewise, ye husbands, dwell with them according to knowledge, giving honor unto the wife, as unto the weaker vessel, and as being heirs together of the grace of life, that your prayers be not hindered. And be not bitter against them. *1 Peter 3:7; Col. 3:19.*

TO WIVES

Wives, submit yourselves unto your own husbands as unto the Lord. *Eph. 5:22.*

Even as Sarah obeyed Abraham, calling him lord; whose daughters ye are, as long as ye do well, and are not afraid with any amazement. *1 Peter 3:6.*

TO PARENTS

And, ye fathers, provoke not your children to wrath, but bring them up in the nurture and admonition of the Lord. *Eph. 6:4.*

TO CHILDREN

Children, obey your parents in the Lord; for this is right. Honor thy father and mother; which is the first commandment with promise: that it may be well with thee, and thou mayest live long on the earth. *Eph. 6:1-3.*

TO SERVANTS, HIRED MEN, AND EMPLOYEES

Servants, be obedient to them that are your masters according to the flesh, with fear and trembling, in singleness of your heart, as unto Christ; not with eyeservice, as men-pleasers, but as the servants of Christ, doing the will of God from the heart; with good will doing service as to the Lord, and not to men; knowing that whatsoever good thing any man doeth, the same shall he receive of the Lord, whether he be bond or free. *Eph. 6:5-8.*

TO EMPLOYERS

And, ye masters, do the same things unto them, forbearing threatening, knowing that your Master also is in heaven; neither is there respect of persons with Him. *Eph. 6:9.*

TO THE YOUNG IN GENERAL

Likewise, ye younger, submit yourselves unto the elder. Yea, all of you be subject one to another, and be clothed with humility; for God resisteth the proud and giveth grace to the humble. Humble yourselves therefore under the mighty hand of God, that He may exalt you in due time. *1 Peter 5:5, 6.*

TO WIDOWS

Now, she that is a widow indeed, and desolate, trusteth in God, and continueth in supplications and prayers night and day. But she that liveth in pleasure is dead while she liveth. *1 Tim. 5:5, 6.*

TO ALL IN COMMON

Thou shalt love thy neighbor as thyself. Herein are comprehended all the Commandments. *Rom. 13:9.* And persevere in prayer for all men. *1 Tim. 2:1.*

Let each his lesson learn with care,
And all the household well shall fare.

SECTION FOUR

Christian Questions with Their Answers

DRAWN UP BY DR. MARTIN LUTHER FOR THOSE WHO INTEND TO GO TO THE SACRAMENT

After Confession and instruction in the Ten Commandments, the Creed, the Lord's Prayer, and the Sacraments of Baptism and the Holy Supper, the pastor may ask, or one may ask himself:

1. **Do you believe that you are a sinner?**

   Yes, I believe it; I am a sinner.

2. **How do you know this?**

   From the Ten Commandments; these I have not kept.

3. **Are you also sorry for your sins?**

   Yes, I am sorry that I have sinned against God.

4. **What have you deserved of God by your sins?**

   His wrath and displeasure, temporal death, and eternal damnation. Rom. 6:21, 23.

5. **Do you also hope to be saved?**

   Yes, such is my hope.

6. **In whom, then, do you trust?**

   In my dear Lord Jesus Christ.

7. **Who is Christ?**

   The Son of God, true God and man.

8. **How many Gods are there?**

   Only one; but there are three Persons: Father, Son, and Holy Ghost.

9. **What, then, has Christ done for you that you trust in Him?**

   He died for me and shed His blood for me on the cross for the forgiveness of sins.

10. **Did the Father also die for you?**

    He did not; for the Father is God only, the Holy Ghost likewise; but the Son is true God and true man; He died for me and shed His blood for me.

11. **How do you know this?**

    From the holy Gospel and from the words of the Sacrament, and by His body and blood given me as a pledge in the Sacrament.

12. How do those words read?

Our Lord Jesus Christ, the same night in which He was betrayed, took bread; and when He had given thanks, He brake it and gave it to His disciples, saying, Take, eat; this is My body, which is given for you. This do in remembrance of Me.
After the same manner also He took the cup when He had supped, and when He had given thanks, He gave it to them, saying, Drink ye all of it; this cup is the new testament in My blood, which is shed for you for the remission of sins. This do, as oft as ye drink it, in remembrance of Me.

13. You believe, then, that the true body and blood of Christ are in the Sacrament?

Yes, I believe it.

14. What induces you to believe this?

The word of Christ, Take eat, this is My body; Drink ye all of it, this is My blood.

15. What ought we to do when we eat His body and drink His blood, and thus receive the pledge?

We ought to remember and proclaim His death and the shedding of His blood, as He taught us: This do, as oft as ye drink it, in remembrance of Me.

16. Why ought we to remember and proclaim His death?

That we may learn to believe that no creature could make satisfaction for our sins but Christ, true God and man; and that we may learn to look with terror at our sins, and to regard them as great indeed, and to find joy and comfort in Him alone, and thus be saved through such faith.

17. What was it that moved Him to die and make satisfaction for your sins?

His great love to His Father and to me and other sinners, as it is written in John 14; Rom. 5; Gal. 2; Eph. 5.

18. Finally, why do you wish to go to the Sacrament?

That I may learn to believe that Christ died for my sin out of great love, as before said; and that I may also learn of Him to love God and my neighbor.

19. What should admonish and incite a Christian to receive the Sacrament frequently?

In respect to God, both the command and the promise of Christ the Lord should move him, and in respect to himself, the trouble that lies heavy on him, on account of which such command, encouragement, and promise are given.

20. But what shall a person do if he be not sensible of such trouble and feel no hunger and thirst for the Sacrament?

To such a person no better advice can be given than that, in the first place, he put his hand into his bosom, and feel whether he still have flesh and blood, and that he by all means believe what the Scriptures say of it in Gal. 5 and Rom. 7.
Secondly, that he look around to see whether he is still in the world, and keep in mind that there will be no lack of sin and trouble, as the Scriptures say in John 15 and 16; 1 John 2 and 5.
Thirdly, he will certainly have the devil also about him, who with his lying and murdering, day and night, will let him have no peace within or without, as the Scriptures picture him in John 8 and 16; 1 Peter 5; Eph. 6; 2 Tim. 2.

NOTE

These questions and answers are no child's play, but are drawn up with great earnestness of purpose by the venerable and pious Dr. Luther for both young and old. Let each one take heed and likewise consider it a serious matter; for St. Paul writes to the Galatians, chapter sixth: "Be not deceived; God is not mocked."

I love God's holy Word, the Bible.
It holds me close
to Jesus, my Savior.

PART TWO

UNIT A

The Existence of God

I BELIEVE IN GOD

HOW WE LEARN ABOUT GOD

There is a God. Every Christian believes this. But also the heathen who have never seen a Bible know there is a SUPREME BEING. This is not surprising, for God has made Himself known.

God speaks to us through the things He has created. The sky, beautiful by day and by night, points us to God. The earth, giving us lovely and useful plants and minerals, reminds us of God. Thousands of living creatures, all of them wonderfully made, prove that there is a God. We learn there is a God when we pause to think about this world.

Every house has a builder; every watch has a maker; every book has an author. Even so this world has a Maker, a Creator, who made the whole world and still preserves it.

We learn about God also through a little voice within us. This little voice is our conscience, which sometimes warns us that there is Someone higher than we are to whom we must answer for our deeds.

The Bible calls that man a fool who says: "There is no God" (Ps. 14:1).

But what we learn about God from nature and from our conscience is not enough. Only in the Bible can we find the full truth about God. In the Bible God Himself tells us exactly who He is and what He has done for us.

1. **How may everyone learn to know about God?**
2. **What does your conscience tell you about God?**
3. **Where only can you learn the full truth about God?**

BIBLE READINGS

God is a Spirit. John 4:24

No man hath seen God at any time. John 1:18

From everlasting to everlasting Thou art, God. Ps. 90:2

I am the Lord, I change not. Mal. 3:6

With God nothing shall be impossible. Luke 1:37

Lord, Thou knowest all things. John 21:17

Do not I fill heaven and earth? saith the Lord. Jer. 23:24

I, the Lord, your God, am holy. Lev. 19:2

The Lord is good to all, and His tender mercies are over all His works. Ps. 145:9

God is Love. 1 John 4:8

BIBLE TEACHINGS

God is the highest Being. He is far above heaven and earth, yet near me at all times. He is without beginning and without end, always the same. I cannot see Him, for He has no body. He is a Spirit. But He is a *personal* Being, with a mind and a will. Even though I cannot see Him, yet I can know Him through His Word.

God can do anything He pleases. He knows everything. He is everywhere in heaven and earth at the same time; therefore I am never alone. God is a perfect Being, without sin. He keeps His promises at all times.

One of the most wonderful truths about God is that He is kind to all His creatures. He loves also me. He uses His wisdom and power for my good. He knows all my troubles and helps me in every need, no matter where I may be.

QUESTIONS AND ANSWERS

1. **Who is the highest Being?**

   God is the highest Being.

2. **How do we know there is a God?**

   Nature, which did not create itself, tells us
   Something within us (conscience) tells us
   Above all, the Bible tells us
   } there is a God.

3. **But why can we not see God?**

   We cannot see God because "God is a Spirit."

4. **What is a spirit?**

   A spirit is a being that has a mind and a will, but is without a body.

5. **How does the Bible describe God?**

   The Bible tells us that God is eternal, unchangeable, almighty, all-knowing, everywhere present, holy, just, faithful, benevolent, merciful, and gracious.

6. **Why do you believe that God is eternal?**

   The Bible says, "From everlasting to everlasting Thou art, God" (eternal).

7. **Why is it always safe to trust God and His works?**

   God does not change; He remains the same (unchangeable).

8. **How great is the power of God?**

   God is almighty; He can help me in every trouble (omnipotent).

9. **Why can nothing be hidden from God?**

   God knows all things, even our most secret thoughts (omniscient).

10. Where is God?

Everywhere; He is always with me (omnipresent).

11. Why can God do no wrong?

God is holy; He loves the good and hates the evil (holy).

12. How does God show that He is just?

God is fair in His dealings with all men (just).

13. Why must we believe that God will always do what He says?

God is faithful; He keeps His promises and His threats (faithful).

14. How is God disposed toward all His creatures?

God is loving and kind; He desires only what is good for them (benevolent).

15. What comfort do we get from knowing that God is merciful?

We are sure that He will abundantly pardon all who are sorry for their sins and believe in Jesus (merciful).

16. Why do you give all glory to God?

God is gracious; He blesses me richly in Christ, without any merit or worthiness in me (gracious).

•WORD STUDY

abundantly: richly, plentifully
conscience: a voice within us which urges us to do what we think is right and warns us against what we think is wrong
to pardon: to forgive
to preserve: to uphold
salvation: giving freedom and life to one imprisoned by sin and death

HYMN STANZA

All praise to God, who reigns above,
The God of all creation,
The God of wonders, power, and love,
The God of our salvation!
With healing balm my soul He fills,
The God who every sorrow stills –
To God all praise and glory! *L. H.*, 19:1

PRAYER

Almighty and everlasting God, I give Thee most humble and hearty thanks that Thou hast made Thyself known unto me; and I beseech Thee, bless my study of Thy Word, that by Thy grace I may know, honor, and praise Thee; through Jesus Christ, Thy Son, my Savior. Amen.

WHAT THIS MEANS TO ME

How comforting it is for me to know that at all times and in all places the holy, almighty God is ever at my side and cares for me with an everlasting love! With Him close to me, I know that all things will work together for my good. I know that this is true because God has told me so in His holy Book, the Bible.

UNIT B

The Triune God

IN THE NAME OF THE FATHER
AND OF THE SON AND OF THE
HOLY GHOST

BIBLE STORY

The Baptism of Jesus Matthew 3:13-17

There was great excitement near the Jordan River. A man dressed in a robe of camel's hair preached with great power. People from all over Palestine hurried out to hear him. He said: "Feel truly sorry for your sins, for the Kingdom of God is here. Therefore be baptized for the forgiveness of your sins."

"Could this be the promised Messiah, who will set up the Kingdom of God?" the people asked. No; it was John the Baptist. He said: "I am only the forerunner of the Messiah. God has sent me to prepare the way for the Lord Christ."

Day after day people from all walks of life came out to hear John preach. He baptized many of them. One day Jesus came and asked to be baptized. Even though He is the holy Son of God, He stood humbly with the lost, the least, and the lowest. He wanted to save the lost, help the least, raise the lowest, and bring them all to the loving Father's heart.

John the Baptist exclaimed: "I need to be baptized of Thee, and Thou comest to me!"

Jesus answered: "Let it be so now, for I must fulfill all righteousness."

Then John baptized Him.

As Jesus came up from the river's edge – wonder of wonders! – the heavens were opened, and the Holy Spirit came down upon Jesus in the form of a dove. At the same time a voice from heaven called: "This is My beloved Son, in whom I am well pleased."

1. **Why was Jesus baptized by John?**
2. **Find the three Persons of the Holy Trinity in the story.**
3. **What words did the pastor use when he baptized you?**

BIBLE READINGS

Hear, O Israel: The Lord, our God, is one Lord. Deut. 6:4

There is none other God but one. 1 Cor. 8:4

The grace of the Lord Jesus Christ and the love of God and the communion of the Holy Ghost be with you all. 2 Cor. 13:14

Go ye, therefore, and teach all nations, baptizing them in the name of the Father and of the Son and of the Holy Ghost. Matt. 28:19

All men should honor the Son, even as they honor the Father. John 5:23

BIBLE TEACHINGS

Our God is wonderful beyond understanding. He is one Being, undivided, and there is no one like Him.

Yet God is three distinct Persons, Father, Son, and Holy Ghost. The Father is true God; the Son is true God; the Holy Ghost is true God. Nevertheless, there are not three Gods, but only one God. Because there are three Persons in God, we call Him the Triune God, or the Holy Trinity.

I cannot understand how this can be, but I believe it because God Himself has told me this in the Bible. I am glad; for all three Persons in God work together for my happiness, as my Creator, my Redeemer, and my Sanctifier.

QUESTIONS AND ANSWERS

1. **Who is the one true God?**

   The one true God is the Triune God, or the Holy Trinity.

2. **What is the Holy Trinity?**

   Three distinct Persons in one God, each Person sharing the power and glory of God equally.

3. **Who are the three Persons in God?**

   The three Persons in God are the Father, the Son, and the Holy Ghost.

4. **Who is the Father?**

   The Father is God and is called the First Person of the Holy Trinity; He is my Creator.

5. **Who is the Son?**

   The Son is God and is called the Second Person of the Holy Trinity; He is my Redeemer.

6. **Who is the Holy Ghost?**

   The Holy Ghost is God and is called the Third Person of the Holy Trinity; He is my Sanctifier.

7. **Why do you believe the doctrine of the Holy Trinity?**

   I believe it because the Bible teaches it.

8. **Why is it most important to believe in the Triune God?**

   This is the true God; only they who believe in Him have eternal life.

WORD STUDY

Sanctifier: The Holy Ghost, who makes us holy through faith in Christ
Creator: Maker, a name usually used for God the Father
Holy Trinity: Father, Son, and Holy Ghost – Three in One
Messiah: Christ, or the Anointed Savior
Redeemer: Savior
Triune: Three in One

HYMN STANZA

Holy, holy, holy! Lord God Almighty!
All Thy works shall praise Thy name in earth and sky and sea.
Holy, holy, holy, merciful and mighty!
God in Three Persons, blessed Trinity!

L. H., 246:4

PRAYER

Dear Lord, who hast made Thyself known to me as the Triune God, Father, Son, and Holy Ghost, I beseech Thee, keep me steadfast in confessing Thee as the one true God; who livest and reignest, ever one God, world without end. Amen.

WHAT THIS MEANS TO ME

I know that the Triune God, Father, Son, and Holy Ghost, is always working together for my happiness. Therefore I will worship, trust, and serve my God with all my soul and with all my mind.

UNIT C

The Bible

THY WORD IS TRUTH

BIBLE STORY

Timothy's Boyhood Training 2 Timothy 1:1-5; 3:14-17

In Lystra there lived a fine, godly boy by the name of Timothy. When he was still a little child, his mother and grandmother told him the wonderful Bible stories that so many people know and love.

From these stories Timothy learned about God and His work of creating the world. He heard what the Scriptures say of God's dealings with His people, such as Abraham, Isaac, and Jacob; Joseph, Moses, and David; and many others.

Especially did Timothy learn that all men are sinners and that God had often promised He would one day send a Savior from sin.

When Timothy had grown to be a young man, the great Apostle Paul visited his home. Paul told him about Jesus, in whom all of God's promises about the Savior had come true. Timothy believed in Jesus with all his heart and made up his mind to become a pastor. Paul loved him as his own son.

Later Paul wrote Timothy two Letters. These are contained in the Bible. In the Second Letter the Apostle wrote: "From a child thou hast known the Holy Scriptures, which are able to make thee wise unto salvation through faith which is in Christ Jesus."

The Letter continues: "All Scripture is given by inspiration of God and is profitable for doctrine, for reproof, for correction, for instruction in righteousness; that the man of God may be perfect, thoroughly furnished unto all good works."

1. **Where did Timothy's mother and grandmother find the stories they told him?**
2. **What were the two main truths Timothy learned?**
3. **From whom did Timothy hear about his Savior, Jesus?**
4. **What may we learn from this story about our Bible?**

BIBLE READINGS

Thus saith the Lord God of Israel. Joshua 24:2

God spake by the mouth of His holy prophets. Luke 1:70

Holy men of God spake as they were moved by the Holy Ghost. 2 Peter 1:21

We speak in the words which the Holy Ghost teacheth. 1 Cor. 2:13

All Scripture is given by inspiration of God. 2 Tim. 3:16

The Scripture cannot be broken. John 10:35

Thy Word is truth. John 17:17

The Holy Scriptures are able to make thee wise unto salvation through faith which is in Christ Jesus. 2 Tim. 3:15

Thy Word is a lamp unto my feet and a light unto my path. Ps. 119:105

Blessed are they that hear the Word of God and keep it. Luke 11:28

BIBLE TEACHINGS

The Bible, or Holy Scripture, is the best book because it is the Word of God. Many holy men of God wrote it, but God gave them the thoughts and the words. Every word comes from God. Therefore every word is true.

The part of the Bible that was written before the birth of Jesus is called the Old Testament. The part that was written after the birth of Jesus is called the New Testament.

In the Bible God tells me about Himself, about the beginning of the world and of man, about sin, and many other important things.

The most wonderful truth God tells me in the Bible is that, out of His great love for me, He gave His Son Jesus to be my Savior from sin. God also tells me in His Word how He wants me to live here on earth.

God wants me to study His Word, to believe it, to love it dearly, and to follow it all my life. Then I shall be truly blessed.

QUESTIONS AND ANSWERS

1. **Which is the best and most important book?**

   The Bible is the best and most important book (the Holy Scriptures).

2. **Why is the Bible the best and most important book?**

   The Bible is the Word of God.

3. **Who wrote the Bible?**

   Many holy men of God wrote the Bible.

4. **Why is the Bible the Word of God although it was written by men?**

   The Bible is the Word of God because God gave these men the thoughts and the words.

5. **How much of the Bible was given or inspired by God?**

   "*All* Scripture is given by inspiration of God."

6. **What must we therefore say of every word in the Bible?**

   We must say that every word in the Bible is true and dependable.

7. **For what purpose did God give us His Word?**

   God gave us His Word so that we might learn how to be saved and how to live a godly life.

8. **What is the foremost doctrine of the Bible?**

   The teaching that Jesus is my Savior is the foremost doctrine of the Bible.

9. **Which part of the Bible was written before the birth of Jesus?**

   The Old Testament was written before the birth of Jesus.

10. **Which part of the Bible was written after the birth of Jesus?**

    The New Testament was written after the birth of Jesus.

11. **How does God want us to use the Bible?**

    God wants us to study the Bible, to believe it, to love it dearly, and to follow it all our lives.

WORD STUDY

divine: belonging to God
doctrine: that which is taught, a teaching
correction: act of making better
inspiration: the act of the Holy Ghost telling men when, what, and how to write
reproof: the act of blaming, or condemning as wrong

HYMN STANZA

How precious is the Book Divine,
By inspiration given!
Bright as a lamp its doctrines shine
To guide our souls to heaven. *L. H.*, 285:1

PRAYER

Blessed Lord, who hast given the Bible to teach me the way to heaven, help me to love that sacred book as my greatest treasure. Fill my heart with Thy Holy Spirit that I may gladly hear and learn Thy Word. May Thy Word be a lamp unto my feet and a light unto my path; through Jesus Christ, my Savior. Amen.

WHAT THIS MEANS TO ME

I will love God's holy Word, the Bible. I will listen attentively whenever it is taught. I will study it and follow everything it tells me. By doing so I shall not only receive God's blessings for my earthly life, but I shall also come closer to Jesus, who is the Way to eternal joy in heaven.

UNIT 1

The First Commandment

THE LORD IS GOD!

Thou shalt have no other gods before Me.

What does this mean?

We should fear, love, and trust in God above all things.

BIBLE STORY

The Giving of the Law Exodus 19 and 20

East of the Red Sea is the land of the Arabs. It is wide, open country, flat and barren. Rising sharply from the plain is a steep mountain, towering a mile high. This is Mount Sinai. Looking at the drowsy quiet that hangs over the mountain and the surrounding wilderness, one would never imagine that anything of importance to us ever happened there.

Yet, about 3,500 years ago, more than a million freed slaves crowded around Mount Sinai to take part in one of the greatest happenings in the history of the world. From the mountaintop came the voice of God Himself: "I am the Lord, thy God, which have brought thee out of Egypt, out of the house of bondage." These words were a friendly greeting from the Lord of heaven and earth to His chosen people, to win their hearts and to make them glad to do His will.

And well they might! For in these words God said to them: "Just think how good I have been to you! I have saved you out of the hands of the Egyptians, who treated you like slaves for so long. I have *proved* to you that I am your God, your Friend and Helper. Now have Me as your God. Worship Me and none other. Do not bow down to the gods of the heathen about you."

While the earth shook and thunder rolled and lightning flashed and smoke blacked out the mountain, God spoke the Ten Commandments, making known His holy will to the people of Israel. Then God wrote the Ten Commandments upon two tablets of stone which Moses was to give to the people. Later God commanded Moses to write the Law in a book. This book is part of the Bible. All people should know and do God's holy will.

1. **Which people gathered around Mount Sinai about 3,500 years ago?**
2. **With which words did God begin talking to His people?**
3. **Read the Ten Commandments in Exodus 20.**
4. **Who makes known His will in the Ten Commandments?**
5. **Why should you know the Ten Commandments?**

BIBLE READINGS

Thou shalt worship the Lord, thy God, and Him only shalt thou serve. Matt. 4:10

I am the Lord; that is My name; and My glory will I not give to another, neither My praise to graven images. Is. 42:8

He that loveth father or mother more than Me is not worthy of Me; and he that loveth son or daughter more than Me is not worthy of Me. Matt. 10:37

The *fear* of the Lord is to hate evil. Prov. 8:13

Thou shalt *love* the Lord thy God with all thy heart and with all thy soul and with all thy mind. Matt. 22:37

It is better to *trust* in the Lord than to put confidence in man. Ps. 118:8

BIBLE TEACHINGS

The only true God is the Triune God: Father, Son, and Holy Ghost. He must have the first place in our heart, for He is our best and dearest Friend. He alone is to be worshiped.

If we worship any other god or any other being, we are worshiping an idol and are sinning against the First Commandment. We do this sin also if we fear any creature more than God, or if we love father or mother, money, food, drink, good times, or anything else, more than God and His Word. We also commit this sin if we trust anyone or anything more than God. *For that to which we give first place in our heart is truly our god.*

The First Commandment is the sum of all. If we could keep this one, we could keep all the others.

If we fear the Lord above all things, we shall do no evil; if we love Him above all things, we shall serve Him only; if we trust in Him above all things, we shall look only to Him for help.

QUESTIONS AND ANSWERS

1. Who is the God to be worshiped by all men?

The Triune God: Father, Son, and Holy Ghost.

2. Why should we worship only the Triune God?

It is only He who gives us life and happiness, the joys of earth, and the hope of heaven.

3. How should we worship God?

We should fear, love, and trust in God above all things.

4. When do we fear God above all things?

When we respect Him so highly that we do nothing against His will.

5. When do we love God above all things?

When we regard Him as our dearest Friend and gladly do His will.

6. When do we trust in God above all things?

When we are sure that He can and will take care of us.

7. What do some people worship instead of the true God?

Some people worship idols.

8. What is an idol?

An idol is any person or thing that receives the fear, love, and trust which belong to God.

9. Why is it sinful to worship idols?

God has forbidden idol worship.

10. Why is it useless to worship idols?

Idols are false gods, who can neither hear nor help us.

11. Of what do many people make idols?

Many people make idols of wood and stone, of food and drink, of money and power, of pleasure and honor.

12. When do we keep the First Commandment?

When we give God first place in our heart.

WORD STUDY

bondage: slavery
confidence: trust
idol: a false god
graven image: carved statue, likeness
worship: the act of showing highest honor to God

HYMN STANZA

Holy, holy, holy! Though the darkness hide Thee,
Though the eye of sinful man Thy glory may not see,
Only Thou art holy; there is none beside Thee,
Perfect in power, in love, and purity.

L. H., 246:3

PRAYER

Almighty and everlasting God, in whom I live and move and have my being, grant, I beseech Thee, that I may fear, love, and trust in Thee above all things; through Jesus Christ, my Redeemer. Amen.

WHAT THIS MEANS TO ME

Ever mindful that the Triune God is my best and dearest Friend, I will always try to serve Him with a godly life and shun everything which is contrary to His holy will. I will pray only to Him for help and worship Him as the only true God. Truly, I will give Him my heart (Prov. 23:26).

UNIT 2

The Second Commandment

GOD'S NAME

Thou shalt not take the name of the Lord, thy God, in vain.

What does this mean?

We should fear and love God that we may not curse, swear, use witchcraft, lie, or deceive by His name, but call upon it in every trouble, pray, praise, and give thanks.

BIBLE STORY

The Ten Lepers Luke 17:11-19

"Jesus, Master, have mercy on us!" was the hoarse, painful cry of ten lepers. Leprosy is a terrible sickness. Lepers were not allowed to be with other people at all. Whenever anyone came near them, they had to cover their faces and cry: "Unclean! Unclean!" They were barred from the city and from going to church with other people. Their sickness was like a living death. Is it any wonder that when they saw Jesus coming, they cried to Him for help?

They had heard of His wonderful deeds and felt sure that He could heal them, even though all doctors had said they could never get well again. They turned to the Lord Jesus for help.

"Go," said Jesus, "show yourselves to the priests." The priests were the public health officers of that time.

The lepers went. At the health station the priest examined them and said: "There is nothing wrong with you."

"But we were lepers," they answered.

"You are lepers no longer," replied the priest; "you have been cured."

How happy they now were! Surely, their thoughts would go back to Him who had made them well!

But only one went back to Jesus. Falling down at Jesus' feet, the man used his now healthy voice to glorify God and thank Jesus for His help. Sadly Jesus asked: "Were there not ten cleansed? But where are the nine? Only this one came back to give glory to God!" Turning to the thankful man, Jesus said: "Arise, go your way. Your faith has made you whole."

1. **Why did ten lepers call on the name of Jesus?**
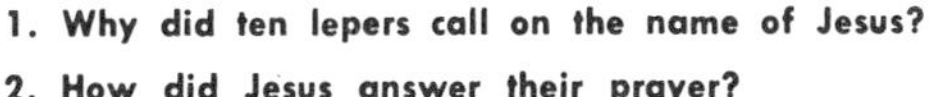
2. **How did Jesus answer their prayer?**
3. **What did nine of the healed lepers forget to do?**
4. **Why did only one of the lepers come back to Jesus?**

BIBLE READINGS

I am the Lord; that is My name. Is. 42:8

Thou shalt call His name Jesus. Matt. 1:21

Whosoever curseth his God shall bear his sin. Lev. 24:15

Ye shall not swear by My name falsely. Lev. 19:12

In vain they do worship Me, teaching for doctrines the commandments of men. Matt. 15:9

Not everyone that saith unto Me, Lord, Lord, shall enter into the kingdom of heaven. Matt. 7:21

The Lord will not hold him guiltless that taketh His name in vain. Ex. 20:7

Call upon Me in the day of trouble; I will deliver thee, and thou shalt glorify Me. Ps. 50:15

Bless the Lord, O my soul, and all that is within me, bless His holy name. Ps. 103:1

It is good to sing praises unto our God. Ps. 147:1

BIBLE TEACHINGS

The name of God tells us who God is, what He is like, and what He has done for us. Therefore His name is very holy and precious. We must not think of using God's name in a sinful way.

It is a great sin to use any name of God in cursing, or joking, or false and careless swearing. People who teach falsely or lead a wicked life and use the name and Word of God to cover up the wrong they are doing, are taking the name of God in vain.

We should remember, however, that God does want us to use His name. In fact, we should use it often. God wants us to think of His love, to tell Him of our needs, and to thank and praise Him in word and song.

QUESTIONS AND ANSWERS

1. What is God's name?

God's name is every name by which God has made Himself known, such as God, Lord, Almighty, Jesus Christ, Holy Ghost.

2. When do we sin against God's name?

We sin against it when we take the name of the Lord, our God, in vain.

3. When is God's name taken in vain?

God's name is taken in vain when we curse, swear, use witchcraft, lie, or deceive by His name.

4. What is cursing?

Cursing is blaspheming God or using the name of God to wish evil upon ourselves or others.

5. What is swearing?

Swearing is calling upon God to witness the truth of what we say and to punish us if we do not tell the truth.

6. When is swearing sinful?

Swearing is sinful when it is done falsely, carelessly, or needlessly.

7. Why is using witchcraft by God's name a great sin?

God's name is used without His permission and promise.

8. How do false prophets lie by God's name?

They preach their own thoughts as if these were the Word of God.

9. How does a hypocrite use God's name in vain?

A hypocrite uses God's name in vain by making others believe that he is a Christian.

10. How should we use God's name?

We should call upon it in every trouble, pray, praise, and give thanks.

11. Why should we call upon God in every trouble?

He is our ever-present Help in every need.

12. How do we remain close to God?

We remain close to God by using His name in frequent prayer.

13. For what should we praise God?

For His wisdom and truth and for His love and mercy.

14. What are we moved to do when we think of God's goodness?

We are moved to thank Him for the great benefits we receive every day.

WORD STUDY

to blaspheme: to speak evil of God or sacred things
to deceive: to mislead
hypocrite: a person who pretends to be better than he is
witchcraft: magic power to do evil

HYMN STANZAS

How sweet the name of Jesus sounds
In a believer's ear!
It soothes his sorrows, heals his wounds,
And drives away his fear.

Jesus, my Shepherd, Guardian, Friend,
My Prophet, Priest, and King,
My Lord, my Life, my Way, my End,
Accept the praise I bring.

L. H., 364:1, 5

PRAYER

Holy, holy, holy is Thy name, O Lord God of Hosts. Help me evermore to keep Thy name holy. Preserve me from saying or doing anything whereby Thy holy name will be dishonored. Grant me Thy Holy Spirit that with my voice and heart and lips I may show forth the honor of Thy name; through Jesus Christ, my Lord. Amen.

WHAT THIS MEANS TO ME

The names which stand for my God are holy and precious to me. I will use them often to sing or speak prayers to Him and to thank and praise Him. God forbid that I should ever use His name thoughtlessly or for shameful cursing or swearing!

UNIT 3

The Third Commandment

GOD'S WORD

Remember the Sabbath day, to keep it holy.

What does this mean?

We should fear and love God that we may not despise preaching and His Word, but hold it sacred and gladly hear and learn it.

BIBLE STORY

The Child Jesus in the Temple Luke 2:41-52

The boyhood home of Jesus was in Nazareth, a little town in Galilee. Each year His parents, Joseph and Mary, went to Jerusalem to take part in the holy Passover festival at the Temple. When Jesus was twelve years old, He went along.

Cheerfully they traveled on, each step bringing them closer to Jerusalem, the holy city of God's

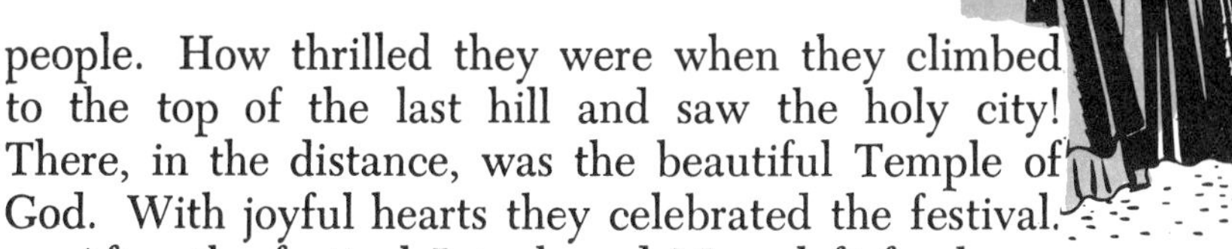

people. How thrilled they were when they climbed to the top of the last hill and saw the holy city! There, in the distance, was the beautiful Temple of God. With joyful hearts they celebrated the festival.

After the festival Joseph and Mary left for home in the company of their friends from Nazareth. Jesus was not with them, but His parents thought He was somewhere in the crowd with other children. Who can describe their feelings when in the evening they discovered that He was not there! Back they rushed to Jerusalem, looking for Him everywhere. Finally, on the third day they found Him in the Temple. He was sitting in the midst of many wise teachers, who were greatly surprised when they noticed how well He knew the Word of God.

Mary cried: "Son, why hast Thou done this to us? Thy father and I were greatly worried, and we looked for Thee everywhere."

Jesus answered: "Why did you look for Me? Did you not know that I must be about My Father's business?"

1. **Why did Joseph and Mary travel to Jerusalem each year?**
2. **How old was Jesus when He went along with them?**
3. **What was it that Jesus found so interesting in the Temple?**
4. **How did Jesus show His love for the Word of God?**
5. **How may we show our love for our church and the Word of God?**

BIBLE READINGS

Let the words of my mouth and the meditation of my heart be acceptable in Thy sight, O Lord, my Strength and my Redeemer. Ps. 19:14

The Son of Man is Lord even of the Sabbath day. Matt. 12:8

Let no man therefore judge you . . . in respect of an holy day . . . or of the Sabbath days. Col. 2:16

Lord, I have loved the habitation of Thy house and the place where Thine honor dwelleth. Ps. 26:8

He that is of God heareth God's words. John 8:47

They continued steadfastly in the Apostles' doctrine and fellowship and in breaking of bread and in prayers. Acts 2:42

Let the Word of Christ dwell in you richly. Col. 3:16

Blessed are they that hear the Word of God and keep it. Luke 11:28

Search the Scriptures. John 5:39

BIBLE TEACHINGS

In the Old Testament the people of God were commanded to keep the Sabbath, the seventh day of the week. They kept the Sabbath by resting from all work and by hearing the Word of God.

Now, in the New Testament, we need no longer keep Saturday or any special day. Yet God wants us to hear His holy Word, to use the Sacraments, and to thank and praise Him. For this purpose we keep Sunday and celebrate Christmas, Easter, Pentecost, and other festivals.

We should also faithfully read the Bible and willingly support those who preach and teach it.

It is sinful to neglect Bible reading or church attendance unless sickness or works of necessity and mercy keep us away.

This is the meaning of the Third Commandment for us Christians.

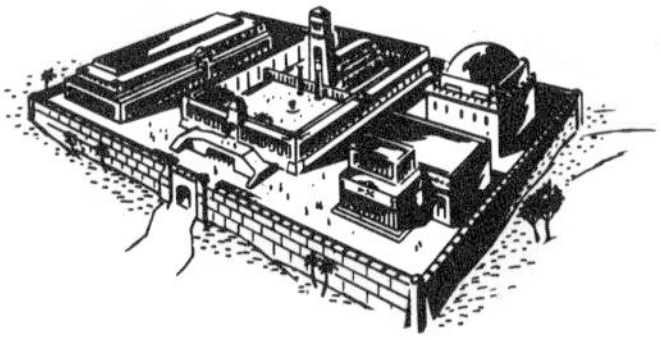

QUESTIONS AND ANSWERS

1. How did God's people in the Old Testament keep the Sabbath day holy?

They rested from their daily work and heard the Word of God.

2. Why are God's people in the New Testament not required to keep the seventh day as a Sabbath?

God has done away with the Old Testament Sabbath.

3. Why do we keep Sunday and celebrate the festivals of the Church?

We keep Sunday and the festivals of the Church so that we may receive God's grace and offer Him our thanks and praise.

4. Why did the first Christian Church choose and appoint Sunday as the day of worship?

Christ rose from the dead on a Sunday.

5. When do we sin against the Third Commandment?

When we neglect to attend church and to read the Bible faithfully.

6. Only what works should keep us from going to church?

Works of necessity and mercy.

7. When do we keep the Third Commandment?

When we come into God's presence to receive His grace in Christ Jesus, and, on our part, offer ourselves to Him in grateful service.

8. How do we receive God's grace in Christ Jesus?

By faithfully using God's Word and Sacraments and believing His promises.

9. How do we offer ourselves to God in grateful service?

By serving the Church, supporting it, and spreading abroad its message.

10. What should prompt us to support the Church and to do good unto all men?

Love for Christ, love for the Church, and love for the unconverted.

11. Why is it that people who profess love for Christ sometimes hold back from supporting His work?

They are thoughtless, selfish, and not duly thankful.

12. Why does the Bible say that people rob God when they do not adequately support the Church?

They withhold from God that portion of time, talents, and treasure which He has a right to expect from His grateful, redeemed children.

13. How should we use all that we are and all that we possess?

We should use all for God's glory and separate a portion for His service.

14. Why should we use all our gifts for the glory of God?

God is the real Owner of everything; we are only stewards, or caretakers.

15. What promises does God give to those who love His Word and support His Church?

"Blessed are they that hear the Word of God and keep it." "Give, and it shall be given unto you."

WORD STUDY

habitation: dwelling; home
meditation: quiet thought
to redeem: to free mankind from sin, death, and the power of the devil
Sabbath: the Old Testament Day of rest and worship

HYMN STANZA

Blessed Jesus, at Thy Word
　We are gathered all to hear Thee;
Let our hearts and souls be stirred
　Now to seek and love and fear Thee,
By Thy teachings, sweet and holy,
Drawn from earth to love Thee solely.

L. H., 16:1

PRAYER

Dear Lord Jesus, who hast said: "Blessed are they that hear the Word of God and keep it," I humbly beseech Thee, grant me Thy Holy Spirit that through my Bible reading at home and the hearing of Thy Word in church and school I may be truly blessed. Let me ever use Thy holy name to sing Thy praises and to show forth the honor of Thy name; through Jesus Christ, my Lord. Amen.

WHAT THIS MEANS TO ME

Hearing and learning God's Word is as important to my soul as food is to my body. Therefore I will feed my soul regularly by faithfully reading my Bible, listening attentively when God's Word is read and taught in family devotions, and by gladly attending church. I know that failure to do so is a sin against God's holy will.

UNIT 4

The Fourth Commandment

PARENTS AND MASTERS

**Thou shalt honor thy father and thy mother,
that it may be well with thee,
and thou mayest live long on the earth.**

What does this mean?

We should fear and love God that we may not despise our parents and masters, nor provoke them to anger, but give them honor, serve and obey them, and hold them in love and esteem.

BIBLE STORY

How Joseph Honored His Father Genesis 47:7-12

Joseph was ruler of Egypt, second only to Pharaoh, the king. All the people of Egypt were commanded to honor and serve him.

For many years Joseph's father, Jacob, was a shep-

herd living in the land of Canaan. When Jacob was very old, Joseph invited him to come down to Egypt and make his home with him. When Jacob came, Joseph hurried out to meet him. He put his arms around his aged father and was so happy that he cried.

Even though Joseph was the great lord of Egypt and his father only a shepherd, Joseph gave his father all the honor and love that he could. He brought his father to the king, who gave Jacob the best of the land for his home.

As long as Jacob lived, Joseph did all that he could to give his father everything he needed and to keep him happy and contented. When Jacob died, Joseph buried him with great honors and deeply mourned him for many days.

1. What position did Joseph have in the land of Egypt?

2. What work did his father Jacob do?

3. How did Joseph show that he loved and honored his father?

4. Think of different ways in which you can make your parents happy.

BIBLE READINGS

Thou shalt love thy neighbor as thyself.
Matt. 22:39

Children, obey your parents in all things. Col. 3:20

Honor thy father and mother; which is the first commandment with promise. Eph. 6:2

Thou shalt rise up before the hoary head and honor the face of the old man. Lev. 19:32

Let every soul be subject unto the higher powers; for there is no power but of God. Rom. 13:1

We ought to obey God rather than men. Acts 5:29

BIBLE TEACHINGS

Father and mother are our best earthly friends. God has given them to be over us in His place. Others whom God has placed over us are our teachers and our government.

It is a great sin against God if we disobey, or despise, or hurt our parents and masters in any way.

The Fourth Commandment says that God wants us to love our father and mother dearly, to thank Him for having given them to us, and to do all we can to give them honor and happiness.

God promises the special blessing of a long and happy life if we gladly do all that His representatives ask of us.

We must not obey, however, when they tell us to do something against God and His Word.

QUESTIONS AND ANSWERS

1. **What does God require of us in the Fourth Commandment?**

   God requires us to honor those who are over us in the home, the church, the school, and the state.

2. **Why must we honor our parents and masters?**

   God has appointed them in His place, as His representatives.

3. **When do we sin against God's representatives?**

   We sin against God's representatives when we despise them, refuse to obey them, or hurt them in any way.

4. **By what actions do children provoke their parents to anger?**

   Children provoke their parents to anger by disobedience and evildoing.

5. **What will become of children who sin against their parents?**

   They will come under the wrath of God.

6. **How would God have us feel and act toward father and mother?**

   We should love father and mother dearly, honor and serve them, and do all we can to make them happy.

7. **Why should we honor father and mother?**

   It is God's will that we do so.

8. What other reasons do we have for honoring father and mother?

Through father and mother God gives us many blessings, for which we should be thankful.

9. How should we show our thankfulness?

We should love our father and mother for all the good that they have done.

10. When especially do our parents need our love?

When they are old, sick, or lonely.

11. What does God promise to children who honor their parents, serve and obey them?

"That it may be well with thee, and thou mayest live long on the earth."

12. Is there ever a time when we must disobey our parents and masters?

Yes; when they tell us to do something against God and His Word.

WORD STUDY

esteem: high regard; thinking highly of someone
hoary: white with age
to provoke: to make angry
representative: one who has the right to act or speak for another
subject: obedient

HYMN STANZAS

Jesus, Savior, wash away
All that has been wrong today;
Help me every day to be
Good and gentle, more like Thee.

Let my near and dear ones be
Always near and dear to Thee;
Oh, bring me and all I love
To Thy happy home above!

L. H., 653:2, 3

PRAYER

Dear heavenly Father, bless my parents and all those whom Thou hast placed over me. Let me never grieve or embitter them. Forgive where I have sinned against them. By Thy Spirit make me willing to give them honor, serve and obey them, and hold them in love and esteem. In Jesus' name I pray. Amen.

WHAT THIS MEANS TO ME

God requires me to serve, obey, love, and honor my father, mother, teacher, government, and all others whom He has placed over me. God would not have me disobey, despise, or hurt my parents and superiors in any way. Out of love for God I will show love to them. For this God promises to bless me.

UNIT 5

The Fifth Commandment

HUMAN LIFE AND WELL-BEING

Thou shalt not kill.

What does this mean?

We should fear and love God that we may not hurt nor harm our neighbor in his body, but help and befriend him in every bodily need.

BIBLE STORY

The Good Samaritan — Luke 10:25-37

The road from Jerusalem down to Jericho was steep and rough. It led through wild mountain country, where robbers could easily hide. One day a traveler walked down this road. Suddenly he was attacked by robbers who took all he had, beat him, and left him half dead.

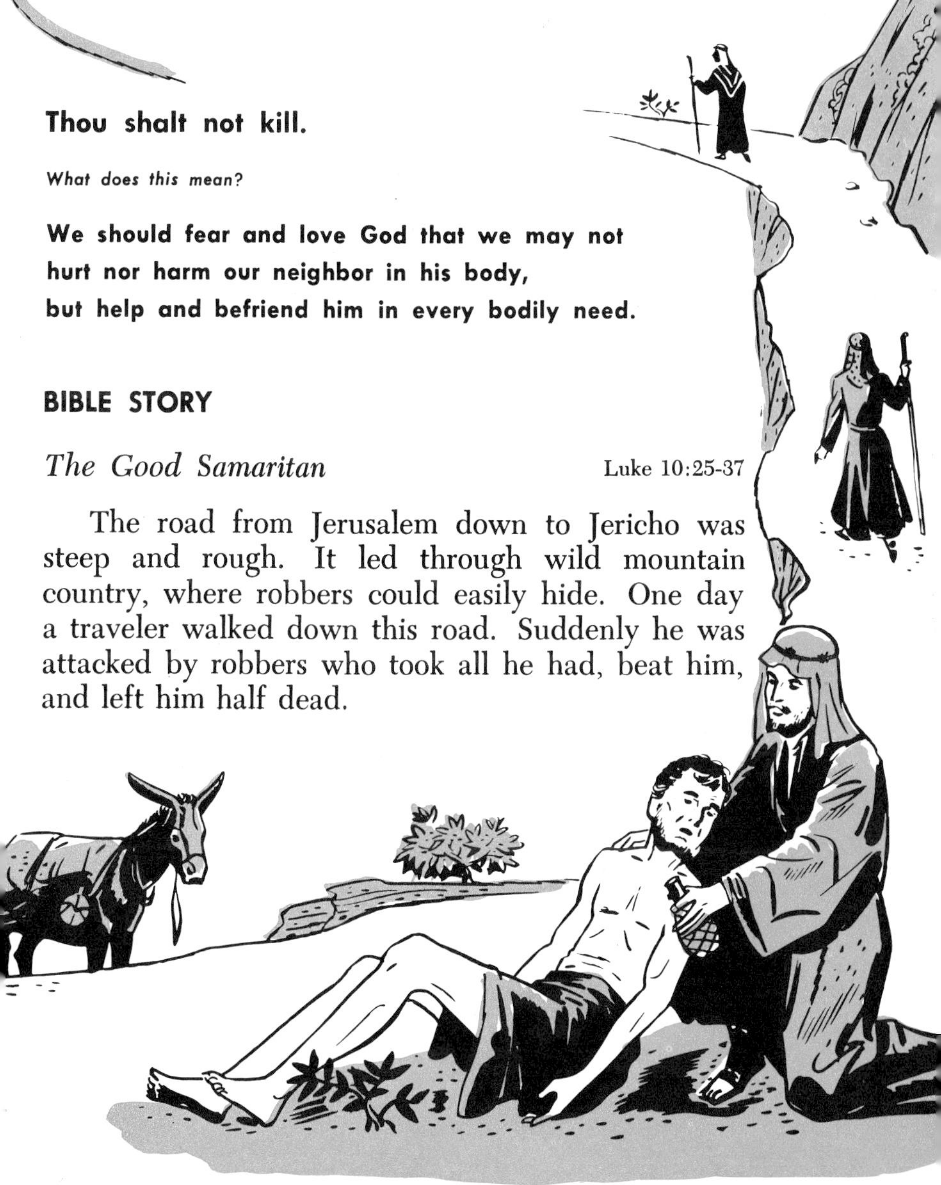

After a while a priest came along the road. When he saw the poor wounded man, he quickly crossed over to the other side and hurried away. Then along came a Levite, a servant in God's Temple. He also took one look at the suffering man and ran away.

Finally, a Samaritan came along. When he saw the bleeding stranger, he stopped at once. First he washed the man's wounds, poured oil and wine on them, and bandaged them. Then he lifted him up on his donkey and brought him to an inn. There he stayed up all night and took care of him.

The next day the Samaritan had to be on his way again. But first he went to the innkeeper and said: "Here is some money. Take care of the man until he is well again. If this is not enough money, I will pay you the rest when I come again."

This is the story Jesus told when a man asked: "Who is my neighbor?"

1. What happened to the traveler?

2. How did the priest and the Levite act toward him?

3. Why was that wrong?

4. How did the Samaritan act?

5. What moved him to help the traveler?

BIBLE READINGS

Whoso sheddeth man's blood, by man shall his blood be shed. Gen. 9:6

Whosoever hateth his brother is a murderer. 1 John 3:15

Out of the heart proceed evil thoughts, *murders.* Matt. 15:19

If thine enemy hunger, feed him; if he thirst, give him drink. Rom. 12:20

Blessed are the merciful, for they shall obtain mercy. Matt. 5:7

Blessed are the peacemakers, for they shall be called the children of God. Matt. 5:9

Love your enemies. Matt. 5:44

Be ye kind one to another, tenderhearted, forgiving one another, even as God for Christ's sake hath forgiven you. Eph. 4:32

BIBLE TEACHINGS

Our life is a very precious gift of God. By the Fifth Commandment God protects human life.

God forbids us to do or say anything by which our own or our neighbor's life may be taken, shortened, endangered, or made unhappy. Even angry thoughts in the heart are murder before God. Only the government has God's permission to punish people to the extent of taking their lives.

As for us, we dare never try to "get even" with any one, or take revenge. We are rather to love all people, even our enemies. We should do all in our power to keep them from being harmed. We should be kind and forgiving toward them.

QUESTIONS AND ANSWERS

1. **What does God forbid when He says, "Thou shalt not kill"?**

   God forbids the sin of hurting our neighbor or ourselves, in body or in spirit.

2. **How is our neighbor hurt or harmed in his body?**

   When we injure him or kill him.

3. **How is our neighbor hurt in his spirit?**

   When we anger him or make him unhappy by the evil we do.

4. **How do we commit murder in our heart?**

   We commit murder in our heart by hating someone.

5. **What does the Bible say of the person who hates another?**

   The Bible says, "Whosoever hateth his brother is a murderer."

6. **When do we injure ourselves in our body?**

   When we neglect our body, overwork it, abuse it, or commit suicide.

7. **Why should we take good care of our body?**

   Our body is a sacred trust from the Lord; we are stewards.

8. Why has only God the right to take human life?

God gave life, and He alone has the right to take it.

9. To whom has God given the right to take human life for the punishment of a crime?

God has given this right to the government.

10. How should we help and defend our neighbor?

We should stand by him when he is in need and seek to further his welfare.

11. Why is it easy to help and befriend those who love us?

They win us by their kindness.

12. Why is it not easy to help and befriend our enemies?

The evil they have done easily moves us to hate them.

13. What requirement does God make of us in the Fifth Commandment?

God asks us to love all people, even our enemies.

14. How should we act toward those who have wronged us?

We should be kind and forgiving to those who have wronged us.

WORD STUDY

to injure: to hurt or harm
remorse: deep sorrow for having done wrong
revenge: returning evil for evil
steward: one who manages another's property
suicide: killing oneself on purpose

HYMN STANZA

In sickness, sorrow, want, or care,
Whate'er it be, 'tis ours to share;
May we, where help is needed, there
Give help as unto Thee!

L. H., 439:5

PRAYER

Loving Savior, take out of my heart all anger and hatred. Teach me to love others as Thou hast loved me. Make me gentle and understanding, kind and forgiving, willing to help my neighbor in every bodily need; through Jesus Christ, my Lord. Amen.

WHAT THIS MEANS TO ME

My neighbor's life and happiness are as important to him as my life and happiness are to me. Therefore I will be kind and forgiving toward him, always keeping in mind the kindness and forgiveness which Jesus shows toward me. I will guard against hatred, envy, quarreling, and any other actions which could make him unhappy.

UNIT 6

The Sixth Commandment

MARRIAGE AND PURITY

Thou shalt not commit adultery.

What does this mean?

We should fear and love God that we may lead a chaste and decent life in word and deed, and each love and honor his spouse.

BIBLE STORY

How Joseph Kept Himself Pure — Genesis 39:1-23

Poor Joseph! He was cruelly treated by his brothers. They hated him so grievously that they wanted to kill him. They actually got rid of him by selling him as a slave. He was brought to Egypt and sold to Potiphar, the captain of the king's guard. There

he was a prisoner in the king's jail, alone and friendless in a strange land.

But the Lord was with Joseph and blessed him. Potiphar thought so much of him that he let him take care of everything he had. All might have been well had not Potiphar's wicked wife desired Joseph and asked him to sin with her. But Joseph said: "No! How can I do this great wickedness and sin against God?"

This made the woman very angry. When her husband came home, she made him believe that Joseph was the one who had done wrong. And that is how Joseph came to be in jail. This seemed to be the worst of all that could happen to Joseph.

But, even in jail, God was still with Joseph. God blessed him in many ways because he had kept himself pure.

1. How was Joseph made a slave?

2. What did Potiphar's wife ask of Joseph?

3. What was his answer?

4. How did God reward Joseph for keeping himself pure?

BIBLE READINGS

What God hath joined together, let not man put asunder. Matt. 19:6

Husbands, love your wives, even as Christ also loved the Church and gave Himself for it. Eph. 5:25

Out of the heart proceed evil thoughts, murders, *adulteries, fornications.* Matt. 15:19

It is a shame even to speak of those things which are done of them in secret. Eph. 5:12

Create in me a clean heart, O God. Ps. 51:10

Keep thyself pure. 1 Tim. 5:22

Flee also youthful lusts. 2 Tim. 2:22

My son, if sinners entice thee, consent thou not. Prov. 1:10

BIBLE TEACHINGS

From the Sixth Commandment we learn that husband and wife may not break the union which God Himself makes when they promise to marry each other. They should be loving and faithful to each other as long as they live.

According to God's will, *all* people, married or unmarried, should be pure in heart, clean in speech, and decent in life.

God's Word, prayer, and work will help us to fight against unclean thoughts and to keep ourselves pure.

QUESTIONS AND ANSWERS

1. **What is marriage?**

   Marriage is the lifelong union between husband and wife.

2. **What does God require of married people?**

   God requires married people to be faithful, loving, and helpful to each other as long as they live.

3. **Of what are they guilty who do not keep the marriage vow?**

   They are guilty of adultery.

4. **What does God expect of all people, young and old, married and unmarried?**

   God expects all people to be pure in heart, clean in speech, and decent in their life.

5. **Why should we stay away from bad companions?**

   Bad companions may lead us into sin.

6. **Why should we avoid everything impure?**

   It will hurt our body and soul, and, above all, it is against God's will.

7. **Whom do we drive away by unclean thoughts, words, and deeds?**

   We drive away God's Holy Spirit and the holy angels.

8. **Why are unclean things often done in secret?**

   Evildoers are ashamed of their unclean deeds and hope to hide them from God and man.

9. **Why is it foolish to think that an unclean deed can be hidden from God?**

   The all-seeing eye of God searches even the most secret places.

10. What is the great purifier of the human heart?

The Word of God is the great purifier of the human heart.

11. How does the Word of God purify our heart?

The Word of God cleanses our heart from all sin and implants love for Jesus.

12. What should be our prayer to check evil desires?

"Create in me a clean heart, O God."

13. What else will help us to lead a chaste and decent life in word and deed?

Diligence, clean play, and the choice of good com panions.

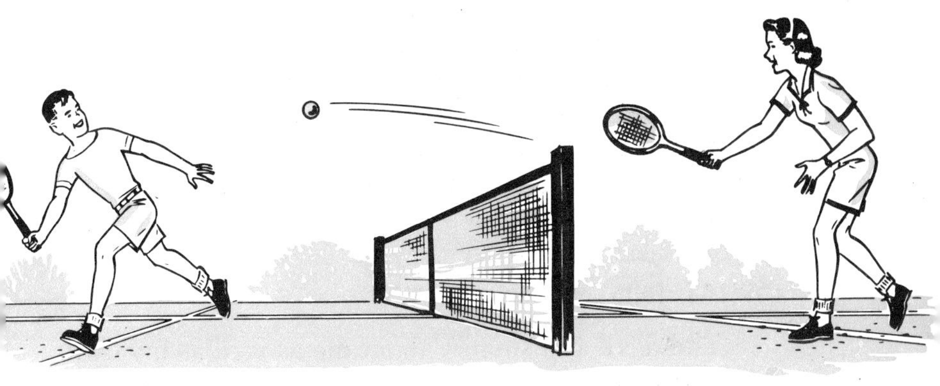

WORD STUDY

adultery: the breaking of the marriage vow
asunder: apart, separate
chaste: clean, pure
fornication: a sinful boy-girl relationship
spouse: husband or wife
vanity: false pride

HYMN STANZA

Grant that our days, while life shall last,
In purest holiness be passed,
  Be Thou our Strength and Tower.
From sinful lusts and vanity
And from dead works set Thou us free
  In every evil hour.
Keep Thou Pure now
From offenses Heart and senses.
Blessed Spirit,
Let us heavenly life inherit.

L. H., 235:8

PRAYER

Create in me a clean heart, O God, and renew a right spirit within me. May I always remember that my body is the temple of the Holy Ghost. Give me strength from above to be pure in thought, word, and deed. O Lord Jesus, make me beautiful within. Amen.

WHAT THIS MEANS TO ME

The devil and sinners about me as well as my own sinful nature are always ready to tempt me to unclean thoughts, speech, and deeds. God's Word, prayer, and work are my best defense against such evils. With God's help I shall set myself against smutty stories, indecent pictures, or, far worse, impure deeds done in secrecy. My motto shall be: "Whatsoever things are pure . . . whatsoever things are of good report . . . I will think on these" (Phil. 4:8).

UNIT 7

The Seventh Commandment

PROPERTY AND BUSINESS

Thou shalt not steal.

What does this mean?

We should fear and love God that we may not take our neighbor's money or goods, nor get them by false ware or dealing, but help him to improve and protect his property and business.

BIBLE STORY

How Achan was Punished for stealing Joshua 7:1-26

The big stone walls of Jericho had just fallen down. Strong as they were, they could not stand up against the power of God. Now God told the people of Israel: "The people of Jericho are very wicked and ungodly. Destroy the city and burn up

everything in it. No one must take anything out of the city.." The people did as God commanded.

Now they moved happily against the next place in Canaan, the small town of Ai. "We shall have no trouble taking Ai," the people said, "because it is much smaller than Jericho, and God is fighting for us. We shall not need our whole army."

But how surprised they were when the people of Ai defeated their army and made them flee! What was wrong? Where was God's help? Sadly their leader Joshua asked God: "O Lord, why didst Thou not help us?"

God answered: "There is one among you who did not obey My command about the things in Jericho. He has stolen some of them. I will not help you so long as that sin is not punished."

The guilty man turned out to be Achan. He had stolen a beautiful coat and some silver and gold and had hidden them in his tent. Achan and his family were stoned to death. Now God again helped His people against their enemies.

1. **Why did God no longer help Israel?**
2. **Why was it wrong for Achan to take a few things found in Jericho?**
3. **How was Achan's sin punished?**

BIBLE READINGS

Ye shall do no unrighteousness in weight or in measure. Lev. 19:35

Out of the heart proceed evil thoughts, murders, adulteries, fornications, *thefts.* Matt. 15:19

The wicked borroweth and payeth not again.
Ps. 37:21

Let him that stole steal no more; but rather let him labor, working with his hands the thing which is good, that he may have to give to him that needeth.
Eph. 4:28

To do good and to communicate forget not.
Heb. 13:16

BIBLE TEACHINGS

In the Seventh Commandment God protects our own and our neighbor's property and business.

It is a sin to steal or to rob. God also forbids every kind of dishonesty, such as giving short weight, overcharging, and underpaying. It is also wrong to waste time at work, to gamble, or to borrow without paying back.

All these sins have their beginning in the selfish, loveless heart.

God wants us to love our neighbor so that we shall gladly help him to keep his property and business, to protect it from harm, and even help him to get more. If our neighbor is poor, we should be happy to share our goods with him.

QUESTIONS AND ANSWERS

1. **What is the most open form of stealing?**

   Robbing another of his money or goods, or forcing from him his property and business.

2. **What are some other forms of stealing?**

   Shortchanging, shoplifting, cheating, overcharging, underpaying, ignoring one's debts, idling at work.

3. **What does God say of a person who aids a thief or knowingly receives stolen goods?**

   God says: "Whoso is partner with a thief hateth his own soul" (Prov. 29:24).

4. **Why is damaging our neighbor's property a form of stealing?**

   We thereby reduce or destroy the value of his property, such as his lawn, shrubs, trees, buildings, desks, tools, or other possessions.

5. **What is the most hidden form of stealing?**

   Wishing to get another's property away from him.

6. **What is our duty if we have found a lost article?**

   We should try to return it to its rightful owner.

7. **What should we do when our neighbor's property is in danger?**

   We should do all we can to protect it.

8. **How should we feel when God blesses our neighbor?**

   We should rejoice with our neighbor.

9. What should we do when our neighbor needs help?

We should help him, even when it is not easy for us to do so.

10. How does God look upon our readiness to help?

He is well pleased.

WORD STUDY

to communicate: to share with others
unrighteousness: wickedness
usury: charging too much interest
ware: goods; merchandise

HYMN STANZA

Grant us hearts, dear Lord, to yield Thee
Gladly, freely, of Thine own;
With the sunshine of Thy goodness
Melt our thankless hearts of stone
Till our cold and selfish natures,
Warmed by Thee, at length believe
That more happy and more blessed
'Tis to give than to receive.

L. H., 442:2

PRAYER

Dear heavenly Father, take out of my heart all desire to steal or to be dishonest. Give me a loving heart to share what I have and to help the poor and needy. Hear me, for Jesus' sake. Amen.

WHAT THIS MEANS TO ME

All stealing is sin, even stealing of small things. I ought particularly avoid dishonesty in small things. To that end I will also guard against such deeds as borrowing without returning, damaging property, and cheating of any kind.

UNIT 8

The Eighth Commandment

GOOD REPUTATION

Thou shalt not bear false witness against thy neighbor.

What does this mean?

We should fear and love God that we may not deceitfully belie, betray, slander, nor defame our neighbor, but defend him, speak well of him, and put the best construction on everything.

BIBLE STORY

How Absalom Spoke Evil Against His Father

2 Samuel 15:1–18:17

Absalom was one of King David's sons. He was very good-looking and was especially proud of his beautiful long hair. He had a selfish, wicked heart and wanted to be king instead of his father. So he tried to take the kingdom away from his father David.

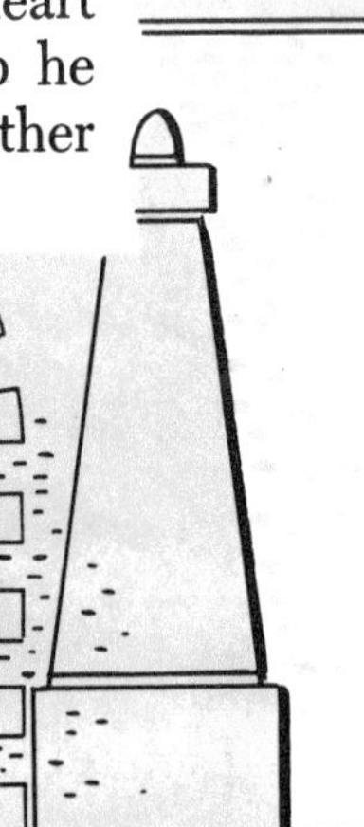

Prince Absalom would stand at the palace gate. When people came to have King David settle some of their troubles, Absalom would stop them and say: "Oh, that I were made judge in the land and every man might come to me! I would deal more fairly with him than my father does." This made many people think that David was not treating them fairly and that it might be better if Absalom were king.

That is how Absalom stole the hearts of the people away from his father David and made him lose his good name.

When Absalom thought he had enough people on his side, he raised an army to fight against his father. David had to flee from Jerusalem, and Absalom made himself king.

But he did not stay king very long. God was angry with him because of his sin. David's faithful soldiers defeated the rebels in a bloody battle, and Absalom himself sped away on his mule. As he rode through the woods, his head got caught in the branches of a big oak tree, and his mule ran right out from under him and left him hanging there. Soon after, one of David's generals found Absalom, and killed him.

1. **How did Absalom make his father lose his good name?**
2. **Would you have acted differently in Absalom's place? Why?**
3. **How was Absalom punished for his sin?**

BIBLE READINGS

Putting away lying, speak every man truth with his neighbor. Eph. 4:25

A false witness shall not be unpunished, and he that speaketh lies shall not escape. Prov. 19:5

Speak not evil one of another, brethren. James 4:11

A talebearer revealeth secrets. Prov. 11:13

Out of the heart proceed evil thoughts, murders, adulteries, fornication, thefts, *false witness.* Matt. 15:19

Let none of you imagine evil in your hearts against his neighbor. Zech. 8:17

Open thy mouth for the dumb . . . and plead the cause of the poor and needy. Prov. 31:8, 9

Charity shall cover the multitude of sins.
1 Peter 4:8

BIBLE TEACHINGS

In the Eighth Commandment, God protects our own and our neighbor's good name, or reputation. A good name is worth much more than riches.

It is a sin against the Eighth Commandment to do or say anything by which our neighbor's good name is hurt or ruined. This is done if we lie about him, give away his secrets, speak evil of him, or keep silent when others speak evil of him.

Love to God and our neighbor will make us defend our neighbor against lies, speak good things about him, and think well of him in our heart.

QUESTIONS AND ANSWERS

1. **How does God seek to protect our neighbor's good name or reputation?**

   God forbids us to do or to say anything that will hurt our neighbor's good name.

2. **Why should we guard even against thinking evil of our neighbor?**

   It is sinful and may lead us to speak evil of him, or to bear false witness against him.

3. **How is our neighbor's reputation hurt or destroyed?**

   This is done when we lie about him, give away his secrets, speak evil of him, or keep silent when others slander him.

4. **Whose child is he who speaks lies?**

   He is a child of the devil, the father of lies.

5. **What will a liar surely receive from God?**

   He will receive punishment from God, for God hates all lies.

6. **What should we do to protect our neighbor's good name?**

   We should defend our neighbor against lies, say good things about him whenever we can, and think well of him.

7. **When especially is our neighbor in need of protection against evil gossip and other forms of false witness?**

   When he is absent and cannot defend himself.

8. How can we put the best construction on our neighbor's words and deeds?

By explaining them in his favor if we can do so in keeping with the truth.

9. What will make us willing to obey God's will in this matter?

The fear and love of God, and love for our neighbor, will make us willing to obey God's will in this matter.

WORD STUDY

charity: Christian love and good will
multitude: a great number
to offend: give a bad example to
reputation: good name, what others think of us
to slander: to spread false reports

HYMN STANZA

Oh, let me never speak
What bounds of truth exceedeth;
Grant that no idle word
From out my mouth proceedeth;
And then, when in my place
I must and ought to speak,
My words grant power and grace
Lest I offend the weak.

L. H., 395:3

PRAYER

O Lord, who art a God of truth and holiness, pour the love of Christ into my heart that I may always speak the truth. Help me to guard my tongue that no false or unkind word may pass over my lips. Grant this, dear Father, for my Savior's sake. Amen.

WHAT THIS MEANS TO ME

God's rule of charity requires that I do all in my power to protect and preserve my neighbor's good name. For this reason I must detest all lies and falsehoods which would injure his reputation. No lie is too small to be a sin in God's sight. I will remember that all lies are of the devil, for he is the father of lies. I will speak well of my neighbor whenever possible.

UNIT 9

The Ninth and the Tenth Commandment

A HOLY HEART

Thou shalt not covet thy neighbor's house.

What does this mean?

**We should fear and love God that we may not
craftily seek to get our neighbor's inheritance or house,
nor obtain it by a show of right,
but help and be of service to him in keeping it.**

**Thou shalt not covet thy neighbor's wife,
nor his manservant, nor his maidservant,
nor his cattle,
nor anything that is thy neighbor's.**

What does this mean?

**We should fear and love God that we may not
estrange, force, or entice away from our neighbor
his wife, servants, or cattle,
but urge them to stay and do their duty.**

BIBLE STORY

How Ahab Got Naboth's Vineyard 1 Kings 21:1-16

King Ahab of Israel had a beautiful summer home near his palace. He was very proud of his fine place and tried to make it more beautiful.

Next to the king's palace was a vineyard, which belonged to Naboth. Naboth liked his vineyard very much, because he had inherited it from his father.

One day King Ahab was very angry. He went to bed, turned his face toward the wall, and would not eat. When his wife, Jezebel, asked him what was wrong, he said: "Naboth has a vineyard which I want very much for a garden. I wanted to pay him for it or give him another vineyard, but he will not let me have it." Naboth had remembered God's command not to sell the inheritance of his father.

Jezebel said: "Are you not the king in Israel? Can you not take what you want? Be of good cheer, I will get Naboth's vineyard for you."

The wicked queen then wrote a letter to the elders of Israel, saying: "Call the people together for a big gathering, set Naboth in a high place before them all, and then let two bad men cry out: 'Naboth has cursed God and the king!' Then carry him away, and stone him that he may die."

The men did as Jezebel told them. Then she hurried to King Ahab and said: "Naboth is dead. Go, and take your vineyard."

1. Why was Ahab angry?
2. Why did Naboth not wish to sell his vineyard?
3. Which of the two men was content with what he had?
4. How did Jezebel help Ahab to get the vineyard?

BIBLE READINGS

The Lord looketh on the heart. 1 Sam. 16:7

The love of money is the root of all evil.
1 Tim. 6:10

Out of the heart proceed *evil thoughts,* murders, adulteries, fornications, thefts, false witness, blasphemies. Matt. 15:19

I had not known lust except the Law had said, Thou shalt not covet. Rom. 7:7

Be content with such things as ye have. Heb. 13:5

Ye shall be holy; for I, the Lord, your God, am holy. Lev. 19:2

BIBLE TEACHINGS

Both the Ninth and the Tenth Commandment say: "Thou shalt not covet." They teach *one* important lesson, namely, that we should not envy our neighbor the things he owns nor wish to get them in a sinful way (covet).

Envy and coveting are truly sins in the sight of God. If not checked, they may lead to such outward evil deeds as lying, stealing, adultery, and even murder.

It is the will of God that our hearts be filled with holy desires only and that we be content with what we have.

QUESTIONS AND ANSWERS

1. **Why do people covet what belongs to others?**

   People covet because of discontent, envy, greed, love of power, and other evil thoughts and desires of the heart.

2. **How does God regard such evil thoughts and desires of the heart?**

   God regards all evil thoughts and desires, no less than words and deeds, as sin.

3. **What may such sinful desires lead to if they are not checked?**

   They may lead to sinful *deeds,* such as murmurings against God, stinginess, dishonesty, cruel treatment of others, as well as stealing, adultery, murder, and war.

4. **Why must all men, even Christians, carefully watch their hearts?**

   All men have evil thoughts and desires in their hearts.

5. **What is the will of God concerning our heart?**

   God wants our heart to be filled with holy desires only.

6. **How do men sometimes seek to get their neighbor's property craftily?**

   They seek to get it by tricks or by foul means.

7. **How do men sometimes seek to get their neighbor's property by a show of right?**

   They make their business deal appear as if they had a right to take the property.

8. **Why does a covetous man always desire more and more?**

   He thinks that having more possessions will make him happy, powerful, and secure.

9. How does God want us to feel about the things He gives to us?

God wants us to be content with such things as He gives us.

10. How does God want us to feel toward our neighbor's property?

God wants us to be happy about our neighbor's welfare and to do all we can to help him keep his property.

WORD STUDY

to covet: to wish to have at the expense of someone else
craftily: in an underhanded and cunning manner
inheritance: property received from parents
to envy: to be discontented at another's good fortune
to entice: to coax away
to estrange: to make unfriendly

HYMN STANZAS

Come, follow Me, the Savior spake,
  All in My way abiding;
Deny yourselves, the world forsake,
  Obey My call and guiding.
Oh, bear the cross, whate'er betide,
Take My example for your guide.

I teach you how to shun and flee
  What harms your soul's salvation,
Your heart from every guile to free,
  From sin and its temptation.
I am the Refuge of the soul
And lead you to your heavenly goal.

L. H., 421:1, 4

PRAYER

Almighty God, unto whom all hearts are open, let Thy Holy Spirit cleanse the secret places of my heart. Help me to avoid every evil thought and wish; preserve me from envy and covetousness. Enable me to rejoice in the prosperity of others, and grant me grace to be content with such things as I have, through Jesus Christ, my Lord. Amen.

WHAT THIS MEANS TO ME

To be envious of others and to covet that which I may not have is sin. I will be satisfied with what God gives me. I will not be envious of others who have things which I do not have. Having food and raiment, I will be therewith content.

UNIT 10

The Close of the Commandments

THE THREATS AND PROMISES OF GOD

What does God say of all these Commandments?

He says thus:

I, the Lord, Thy God, am a jealous God,

visiting the iniquity of the fathers upon the children

unto the third and fourth generation of them that hate Me,

and showing mercy unto thousands of them that love Me

and keep My Commandments.

What does this mean?

God threatens to punish all that transgress these Commandments.

Therefore we should fear His wrath and not act contrary to them.

But He promises grace and every blessing to all that keep these Commandments.

Therefore we should also love and trust in Him and willingly do according to His Commandments.

BIBLE STORY

The Fall into Sin

Genesis 3:1-24

Adam and Eve were perfectly happy. God had done everything to make them enjoy every moment of their life. He had created them pure and holy. He had built a beautiful park, or paradise, to be their home. There God came and talked with them. They could have His blessed company at all times. What more could they want?

God asked only one thing of them: "You may eat the fruit of all the trees in the garden except the one in the center. If you eat of that, you shall surely die."

One day Satan, the leader of the bad angels, set out to take all happiness away from Adam and Eve. He came into the garden in the form of a serpent and said to Eve: "Did God really say that you may not eat of every tree in the garden? It will not hurt you at all. God simply does not want you to be as wise as He is."

Eve listened to the devil's lies and ate some fruit of the forbidden tree. Then she gave some to Adam

also, and he ate. Hardly had they tasted the fruit when they found out that the devil had deceived them. Now they knew that they had done the one thing God had told them not to do. They saw that all was lost, and they were ashamed and afraid of God.

God was angry and drove Adam and Eve out of their wonderful home. From that day on they had much suffering and sorrow because of their sin, and finally they would have to die.

Yet God still loved them. At once He promised them the Savior who should break the devil's power and save all people from their sins.

1. Tell what God had done to make Adam and Eve happy.
2. What had God told them they must not do?
3. Why did they not obey God's command?
4. How were they punished for their sin?
5. How did God show His great love even after Adam and Eve had sinned?

BIBLE READINGS

The imagination of man s heart is evil from his youth. Gen. 8:21

The soul that sinneth, it shall die. Ezek. 18:20

By one man sin entered into the world, and death by sin. Rom. 5:12

The wages of sin is death. Rom. 6:23

Be not deceived; God is not mocked. Gal. 6:7

I will put enmity between thee and the woman, and between thy seed and her Seed; It shall bruise thy head, and thou shalt bruise His heel. Gen. 3:15

Godliness is profitable unto all things, having promise of the life that now is and of that which is to come. 1 Tim. 4:8

BIBLE TEACHINGS

God gave His Commandments to all people. He wants everyone to obey His Commandments altogether. He is a *jealous* God; that is, He wants every Commandment kept perfectly, in thought, word, and deed.

God hates every single sin, even sinful thoughts. If the sinner does not repent, God will punish him with eternal death. Such punishment is fully deserved because every sin is something done against God's holy will. This truth should make us afraid of God's anger and careful not to do anything against His Commandments.

On the other hand, God promises to bless all those who love Him and keep His Commandments. This truth should make us willing to obey Him.

QUESTIONS AND ANSWERS

1. **What does God say of Himself in the conclusion of the Commandments?**

   He says, "I, the Lord, thy God, am a jealous God."

2. **Why does God call Himself a jealous God?**

   He expects us to love and obey Him only.

3. **Why does God have the right to expect obedience?**

   He is the Lord of all, and the rightful Lawgiver.

4. **How does God want His Commandments to be kept?**

   God wants His commandments to be kept perfectly in thought, word, and deed.

5. **Of what are they guilty who do not keep God's Commandments perfectly?**

   They are guilty of sin.

6. **From whom have all children inherited sin?**

   All children have inherited sin from Adam through their parents.

7. **How have they added to the sin of Adam?**

   They daily commit sinful acts.

8. **How does God show His anger toward those who sin?**

   He visits iniquity upon such persons; that is, He punishes them.

9. **How severely does He punish them?**

   He visits the iniquity of the fathers upon the children unto the third and fourth generation.

10. **What should God's great anger over sin move us to do?**

    We should fear His wrath and not act contrary to His Commandments.

11. What does God show unto them that love Him and keep His Commandments?

He shows mercy unto thousands of them that love Him and keep His Commandments.

12. What should God's blessing upon obedience move us to do?

We should love God and trust in Him and willingly do according to His Commandments.

WORD STUDY

to assail: to attack
to bruise: to hurt, to crush
enmity: ill will, hatred
generation: people born in the same period of time
grace: undeserved mercy and kindness
imagination: the thoughts and feelings
jealous: requiring complete obedience

HYMN STANZA

Lord Jesus, who dost love me,
Oh, spread Thy wings above me
And shield me from alarm!
Though evil would assail me,
Thy mercy will not fail me:
I rest in Thy protecting arm.

L. H., 554:5

PRAYER

I confess to Thee, God Almighty, the Father, the Son, and the Holy Spirit, that I have sinned in thought, word, and deed, through my fault, my own fault, my own most grievous fault; wherefore I pray Thee, Almighty God, to have mercy upon me, to forgive me all my sins, and to make clean my heart within me. – Almighty and merciful Lord, grant me pardon and forgiveness of all my sins, space for true repentance, amendment of life, and the grace and comfort of the Holy Spirit! Amen.

WHAT THIS MEANS TO ME

God expects me to obey all His Commandments. He knows all my sins, and holds me accountable for every single sin, even my sinful thoughts. Unless I repent of my sins and beg His forgiveness, He will punish me with eternal death. I must therefore avoid making Him angry by disobeying His will. Out of love for Him I will gladly keep His Commandments. Then He will surely bless me.

UNIT 11

The Close of the Commandments

THE PURPOSE OF THE LAW

BIBLE STORY

The Rich Young Ruler

Mark 10:17-22

One day a rich young man came running to Jesus. He asked: "Good Master, what good thing shall I do that I may have eternal life?"

Jesus answered: "You know the Commandments. Keep them, and you shall go to heaven."

"Which Commandments?" the young man asked.

Jesus told him: "Do not commit adultery; do not kill; do not steal; do not bear false witness; honor your father and your mother; love your neighbor as yourself."

"Oh," cried the young man, "I have kept all of those since I was a child! What else do I need?"

Jesus looked at him lovingly and answered: "The one thing you need is to sell all your property, give the money to the poor, and follow Me. Then you shall have treasure in heaven."

The young man heard what Jesus told him. He had nothing to say. He loved his money above all. He sadly walked away.

1. **How did the rich young man hope to obtain eternal life?**
2. **What wrong opinion did he have of himself?**
3. **Why did Jesus ask the young man to sell his property?**

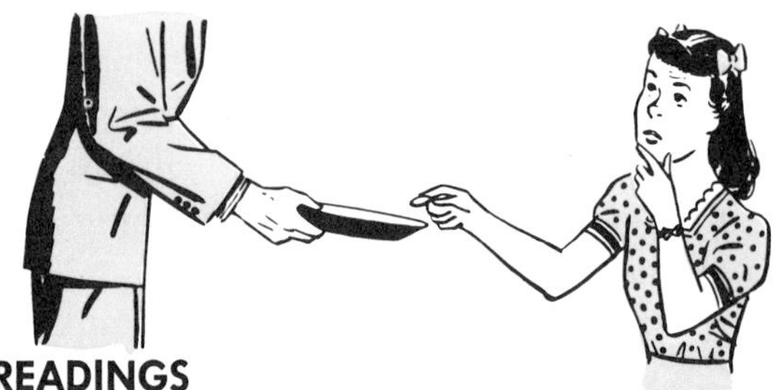

BIBLE READINGS

The Law is holy and just and good. Rom. 7:12

The Law is made for the lawless and disobedient. 1 Tim. 1:9

A corrupt tree bringeth forth evil fruit. Matt. 7:17

By the Law is the knowledge of sin. Rom. 3:20

I know that in me (that is, in my flesh) dwelleth no good thing. Rom. 7:18

Wherewithal shall a young man cleanse his way? By taking heed thereto according to Thy Word. Ps. 119:9

Christ hath redeemed us from the curse of the Law, being made a curse for us. Gal. 3:13

BIBLE TEACHINGS

The Law is holy and good because it comes from God. But it cannot make us holy or lead us to heaven. We cannot keep the Commandments as God wants us to keep them. To keep the Law we must love God with all our heart. We are all sinful, however, and cannot love God with all our heart.

Yet the Law of God serves a very necessary and useful purpose. First, it prevents many wicked deeds. Second, the Law acts like a mirror. It shows us how we look in the sight of God – evil in thought, word, and deed. It shows us that we are lost and condemned and that we cannot save ourselves. Finally, the Law is a rule, showing us how God wants us to live in order to please Him.

Our Savior Jesus Christ has redeemed us from all our sins against the Law of God and from its curse.

QUESTIONS AND ANSWERS

1. What must you confess now that you have studied the Ten Commandments?

I must confess that I have sinned in thought, word, and deed through my own fault.

2. What have you deserved because of your transgressions?

I have deserved God's wrath and punishment.

3. Why do you hope to be saved despite your many transgressions?

Christ has redeemed me from the curse of the Law, being made a curse for me (Gal. 3:13).

4. Where do you learn that you are freed from the curse of the Law?

I learn this from the Gospel.

5. What is the Gospel?

The Gospel is the glad news that Jesus kept the Law for me and died for my sins.

6. Why will you always need strength from above to walk in the way of the Lord?

I know that in me, that is, in my flesh, dwelleth no good thing (Rom. 7:18).

7. Why may you hope to keep the Commandments better in the future?

It is God who maketh me both to will and to do the things which are acceptable unto His divine majesty (Phil. 2:13).

8. Where in the Catechism do you learn the Gospel?

I learn the Gospel in the Second Chief Part of the Catechism.

9. Of what value has the study of the First Chief Part been to you?

I learned to know that the Law serves as a curb, a mirror, and a rule.

10. In what way does the Law serve as a curb?

The Law checks the coarse outbursts of sin.

11. In what way does the Law serve as a mirror?

"Through the Law is the knowledge of sin" (Rom. 3:20).

12. In what way does the Law serve as a rule?

It shows the Christian the life that pleases God.

13. Who is the Way to life everlasting?

The Lord Jesus Christ is the Way, the Truth, and the Life.

14. Where in the Catechism do we learn of this way?

In the Apostles' Creed.

WORD STUDY

corrupt: rotten, wicked
lawless: paying no attention to the law
precepts: commandments, rules
to prevent: to keep from happening
to redeem: to buy back, to make free
transgression: breaking of the law, sin

HYMN STANZA

May we Thy precepts, Lord, fulfill
And do on earth our Father's will
  As angels do above;
Still walk in Christ, the living Way,
With all Thy children and obey
  The law of Christian love.

L. H., 412:1

PRAYER

O holy and righteous God, Thy Law has shown me my sinful and lost condition. Have mercy on me, and forgive me all my sins for Jesus' sake. Out of a thankful heart let me love Thee with all my strength and do those things which are pleasing unto Thee; through Jesus Christ, my Savior. Amen.

WHAT THIS MEANS TO ME

God's Law, the Ten Commandments, is my true guide to God-pleasing living. I must learn it, study it, and keep it ever before my eyes and heart, so that I can faithfully walk in God's path. But I can never keep God's Law perfectly. How thankful I ought to be that He sent Jesus to keep the Law for me and earn forgiveness for my sins!

UNIT 12

THE FIRST ARTICLE — CREATION

God, the Creator

"The Earth Is the Lord's and the Fullness Thereof"

**I believe in God the Father Almighty,
Maker of heaven and earth.**

What does this mean?

I believe that God has made me and all creatures;

that He has given me my body and soul, eyes, ears, and all my members,

my reason and all my senses, and still preserves them;

also clothing and shoes, meat and drink, house and home,

wife and children, fields, cattle, and all my goods;

that He richly and daily provides me with all that I need

to support this body and life;

that He defends me against all danger,

and guards and protects me from all evil;

and all this purely out of fatherly, divine goodness and mercy,

without any merit or worthiness in me;

for all which it is my duty to thank and praise, to serve and obey Him.

This is most certainly true.

How God Made All Things Genesis 1

In the beginning God created the heaven and the earth.

First of all, God made light and divided the light from the darkness. He called the light Day and the darkness Night. So ended the very first day in the history of the world.

During the next five days God placed new creatures into the world. On the second day He parted the water in the sky from the water on earth and made the blue heavens to keep them apart. On the third day God made the oceans, lakes, and rivers, and put them in their places, and commanded the dry land to appear. Then He covered the earth with a fresh and lovely green: grass, shrubs, flowers, shade trees, and fruit trees. The next day God made the skies beautiful with heavenly lights of all kinds, the sun, the moon, and the stars.

So far there were no animals. But now, on the fifth day, God made the wonderful creatures that live in the water and in the air, such as fishes and whales and birds of all sizes and colors.

The sixth day was the greatest of all. In it God made all the different kinds of animals that live on land, creeping, or jumping, or running. And, last and best of all, God made the first people, a man and a woman.

God looked on everything He had made and saw that it was very good. God's work of creation was finished. On the seventh day God rested.

1. **How was the world made?**
2. **Tell what God made in the first six days of the world.**
3. **Which was the last and best of God's visible creatures?**

BIBLE READINGS

In the beginning God created the heaven and the earth. Gen. 1:1

By Him were all things created, visible and invisible. Col. 1:16

By the Word of the Lord were the heavens made. Ps. 33:6

Through faith we understand that the worlds were framed by the Word of God. Heb. 11:3

My help cometh from the Lord, which made heaven and earth. Ps. 121:2

I trusted in Thee, O Lord; I said, Thou art my God. Ps. 31:14

BIBLE TEACHINGS

In the Bible we learn about many works of God.

The first work of God mentioned in the Bible is the creation of the world. In the beginning God, by His almighty Word, made all things out of nothing. This great and mighty God is my loving Father through Christ, my Savior. In Him will I trust for every good thing.

QUESTIONS AND ANSWERS

1. Which part of the Catechism tells us about the work of the Triune God?

The Apostles' Creed.

2. What is a creed?

A creed is a brief summary of what we believe.

3. Why is the oldest Christian Creed called the Apostles' Creed?

It presents the main teachings of the Apostles.

4. What are the main teachings of the Apostles?

God the Father is the Creator, God the Son is the Redeemer, and God the Holy Ghost is the Sanctifier.

5. How is the Apostles' Creed a beautiful picture of the Holy Trinity?

There is one Creed but Three Articles, even as there is one God but Three Persons.

6. Why do you call the First Person of the blessed Trinity the Father?

He is the Father of Jesus Christ and the Maker and Preserver of all things.

7. Of what did God make heaven and earth?

God made heaven and earth out of nothing.

8. How is it possible that all things could be made of nothing?

"Our God is in the heavens; He hath done whatsoever He hath pleased." Ps. 115:3.

9. Why can our God do whatsoever He has pleased to do?

God is almighty. He has created everything by the Word of His power.

10. Why do we believe this?

God has said so, and we trust in His Word.

11. What two kinds of creatures has God made?

He has made visible and invisible creatures.

12. To whom do you belong by right of creation?

I belong to God, for I am His workmanship.

13. Why do you count it a privilege to live and serve your Creator?

He is my dear Father in Christ, my Savior.

WORD STUDY

adoration: worship
creature: something God has made
invisible: not capable of being seen
to preserve: to uphold, to protect
privilege: favor, honor
throng: large number of persons
visible: capable of being seen

HYMN STANZA

Praise to the Lord, the Almighty, the King of creation!
O my soul, praise Him, for He is thy Health and Salvation!
Join the full throng;
Wake, harp and psalter and song;
Sound forth in glad adoration!

L. H., 39:1

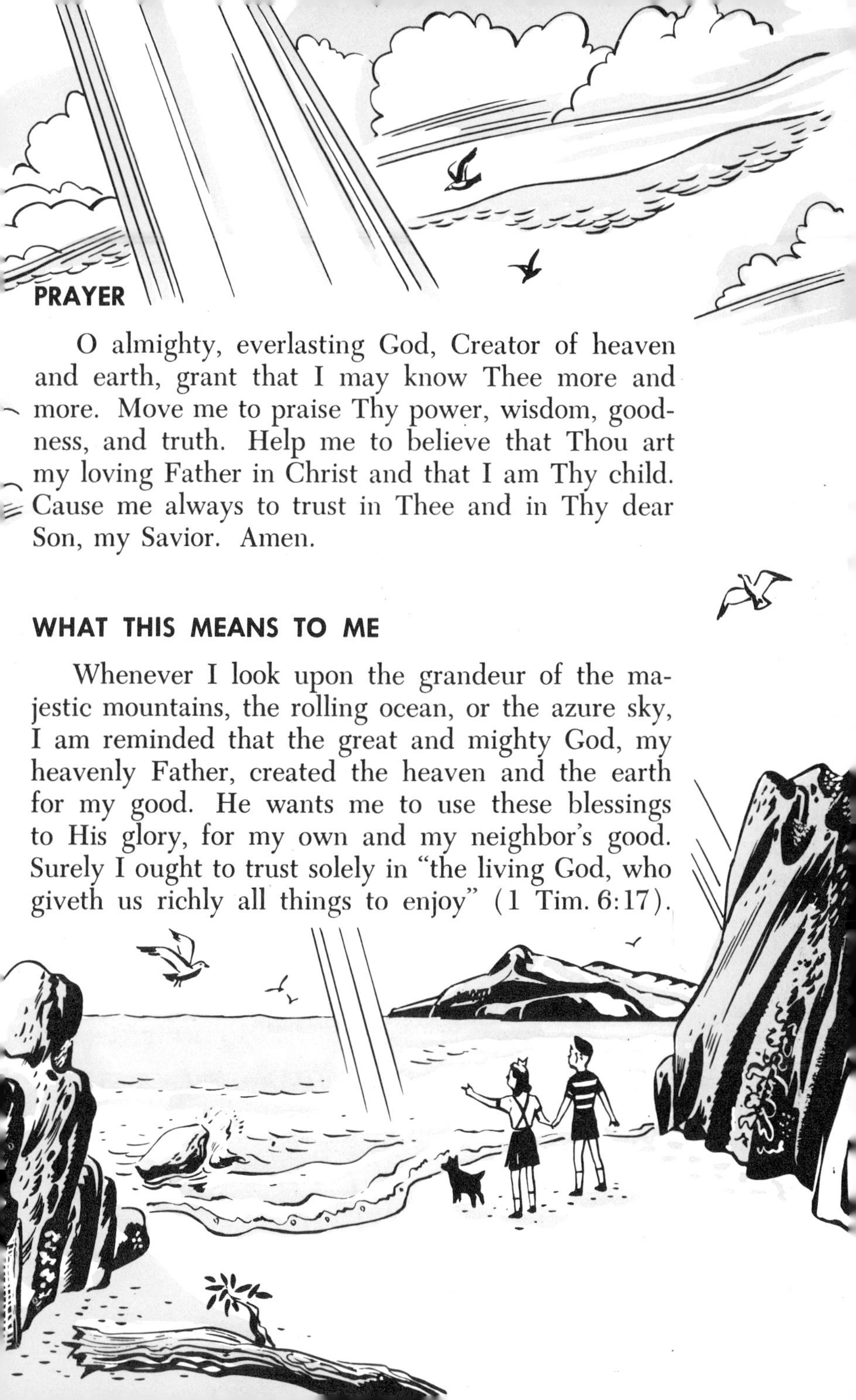

PRAYER

O almighty, everlasting God, Creator of heaven and earth, grant that I may know Thee more and more. Move me to praise Thy power, wisdom, goodness, and truth. Help me to believe that Thou art my loving Father in Christ and that I am Thy child. Cause me always to trust in Thee and in Thy dear Son, my Savior. Amen.

WHAT THIS MEANS TO ME

Whenever I look upon the grandeur of the majestic mountains, the rolling ocean, or the azure sky, I am reminded that the great and mighty God, my heavenly Father, created the heaven and the earth for my good. He wants me to use these blessings to His glory, for my own and my neighbor's good. Surely I ought to trust solely in "the living God, who giveth us richly all things to enjoy" (1 Tim. 6:17).

UNIT 13

THE FIRST ARTICLE — CREATION

The Story of the Angels

"Bless the Lord, Ye His Angels"

BIBLE STORY

How an Angel Protected the Three Men in the Fiery Furnace Daniel 3:1-28

Mighty King Nebuchadnezzar of Babylon had fought against the kingdom of Judah and had defeated it. He took many of the people of Judah along to Babylon as prisoners. They now had to live in that strange land.

Among the prisoners were three friends whose names were Shadrach, Meshach, and Abednego.

They were godly young men and faithfully worshiped the true God, even though they lived among the heathen people of Babylon.

King Nebuchadnezzar made a large golden image, or statue, and said: "I command all people to fall down and worship this statue. Anyone that does not do so shall be thrown into a very hot furnace." Most of the people obeyed the king.

But the three friends would not fall down and worship the statue. They told the king: "We are not afraid of your fiery furnace. Our God, whom we serve, is able to deliver us from the fire. We will not worship your golden image."

The king was very angry and ordered them to be thrown into the furnace, which was fired seven times hotter than usual. Nebuchadnezzar then watched to see the three men burn up.

"What is this?" cried the king. "Did we not put three men into the fire? I see four men walking around in the flames, and the fourth is like unto the Son of God." Quickly he called to them to come out of the furnace. They were not touched by the fire. There was not even the smell of smoke on their clothes.

Then Nebuchadnezzar said: "Blessed be the God of Shadrach, Meshach, and Abednego, who has sent His angel and delivered His servants that trusted in Him."

1. **What did King Nebuchadnezzar order all the people to do?**
2. **What did he threaten to do to those who would not obey?**
3. **Why did the three friends refuse to obey the king's command?**
4. **What was done with them?**
5. **Why were they unharmed?**

BIBLE READINGS

Are they [the good angels] not all ministering spirits, sent forth to minister for them who shall be heirs of salvation? Heb. 1:14

The Son of Man shall come in His glory, and all the holy angels with Him. Matt. 25:31

The Lord shall give His angels charge over thee to keep thee in all thy ways. Ps. 91:11

God spared not the angels that sinned, but cast them down to hell. 2 Peter 2:4

The devil was a murderer from the beginning; he is a liar. John 8:44

Be sober, be vigilant, because your adversary, the devil, as a roaring lion, walketh about, seeking whom he may devour. 1 Peter 5:8

BIBLE TEACHINGS

The angels are the greatest of God's invisible creatures. There are good angels and bad angels.

The good angels are *holy* spirits. There are very many of them, and they are very powerful. Their work is to praise God, to carry out His commands, and to serve and protect His children.

The bad angels, too, were created holy, but they fell away from God and were sent to hell. There are very many bad angels also, and they are powerful and cunning. Their leader is Satan. The bad angels spend their time trying to lead God's children into sin and damnation.

QUESTIONS AND ANSWERS

1. **Which are the foremost among God's invisible creatures?**
   The angels are the foremost among God's invisible creatures.

2. **Why are the angels invisible?**
   They are spirits, without flesh and blood.

3. **What does the Bible tell us of the good angels?**
   The Bible tells us that the good angels are holy, very numerous, and very powerful.

4. **What blessing do the good angels enjoy?**
   They see God face to face.

5. **What great service do they render God?**
   They carry out the commands of God and praise Him.

6. **What great service do they render God's children?**
   They protect them from harm and danger.

7. Why are you happy to know of the good angels?

The good angels are sent by my heavenly Father to watch over me.

8. When are the good angels around us?

When we walk in God's ways.

9. Who is near when we do not walk in God's ways?

The evil angels are near when we do not walk in God's ways.

10. Why are they evil?

They fell away from God and turned their mind and will against Him.

11. How did God punish the evil angels?

He cast them out of their heavenly home and sent them into hell for everlasting punishment.

12. What is the dread purpose of Satan and his evil angels?

To separate us from God by making us to sin.

13. How can we be safe from Satan?

By trusting in God, using His Word, and walking in His ways.

WORD STUDY

adversary: enemy
cunning: sly, tricky
to devour: to swallow up
image: statue
to minister: to help, to serve
vigilant: watchful

HYMN STANZA

Lord, give Thy angels every day
Command to guide us on our way,
And bid them every evening keep
Their watch around us while we sleep.
L. H., 256:3

PRAYER

Heavenly Father, grant, I pray Thee, that Thy holy angels may protect and guard me from all evil. Give them charge over me that the evil angels may not harm me. Hear me for Jesus' sake. Amen.

WHAT THIS MEANS TO ME

How comforting it is for me to know that my loving Father in heaven sends His holy angels to serve and protect me in all my ways! For this kindness I ought to thank God daily and ask Him to keep His guardian angel ever at my side.

But I must not forget that Satan's bad angels are ever present, too. Each day I ought to pray God to protect me against their wicked temptations.

UNIT 14

THE FIRST ARTICLE — CREATION

The Story of Man

"God hath Made of One Blood All Nations of Men"

BIBLE STORY

How God Created Adam and Eve

Genesis 1:26-31; 2:1-25

It was the sixth day of the world. God had made all of His creatures except one.

Now God took some earth and formed it in the shape of a man. Then He breathed into his nostrils, and the man became alive. God gave the man a soul that can never die, and also the power to think. Best of all, God made man holy and without sin, like Himself. The name of this first man was Adam.

Soon afterwards God let Adam see all the animals which He had made, but Adam found none that could be a real partner for him. So God put Adam to sleep, took a rib from his body, and made a woman out of the rib. God brought her to Adam to be his wife, and Adam called her Eve.

A beautiful park, called the Garden of Eden, was the home which God made for Adam and Eve. It was full of wonderful fruit trees. Here Adam and Eve could live, perfectly holy and perfectly happy, and rule over the wonderful world God had created.

1. **When did God create the first man?**
2. **Show in what ways Adam and Eve were higher creatures than the animals.**
3. **In what way were Adam and Eve like God?**
4. **Why were Adam and Eve perfectly happy when God made them?**

BIBLE READINGS

The Lord God formed man of the dust of the ground and breathed into his nostrils the breath of life; and man became a living soul. Gen. 2:7

God said, Let us make man in Our image, after Our likeness, and let them have dominion . . . over all the earth. Gen. 1:26

I am . . . wonderfully made; marvelous are Thy works. Ps. 139:14

Put on the new man, which after God is created in righteousness and true holiness. Eph. 4:24

BIBLE TEACHINGS

God's greatest visible creature is man. God formed his body out of the earth, gave him a soul that can never die, and made him able to think. God also made man ruler over all the earth. Best of all, God created man in His own image; that is, God made man perfectly holy, like Himself.

QUESTIONS AND ANSWERS

1. **Why did God give particular attention to the creation of man?**

   Man was to be the best and foremost of all visible creatures.

2. **How did God make the first human body?**

   God formed the first human body of the dust of the ground.

3. **How did God give man a special kind of life?**

   "God breathed into his nostrils the breath of life, and man became a living soul."

4. **How did God enable man to rule over all the earth?**

   God provided man with reason, which enables man to think.

5. **How did Adam, the first man, show the wonderful power of his mind?**

   Adam correctly named every creature of God.

6. **Whom did God create as a companion for Adam?**

   God created Eve.

7. **Why did Adam name his wife Eve?**

   She was to be the mother of all the living.

8. **What was the greatest blessing given to Adam and Eve?**

   Adam and Eve were created in the image of God.

9. **How did the divine image make Adam and Eve the best and foremost of all visible creatures?**

   They were like God, holy and righteous; they knew God and were happy in this knowledge.

10. **What was to be the chief work of our first parents in the Garden of Eden?**

    In their daily work they were to glorify God for His goodness and were to rule over God's creatures.

WORD STUDY

dominion: rule
image: likeness
marvelous: wonderful
yield: bring forth

HYMN STANZA

The Lord, my God, be praised,
My Light, my Life from heaven;
My Maker, who to me
Hath soul and body given;
My Father, who doth shield
And keep me day by day,
Doth make each moment yield
New blessings on my way.

L. H., 38:1

PRAYER

O God, almighty Creator of all things, I praise Thee for Thy marvelous works; Thou hast wonderfully made me. Grant me strength and grace at all times to serve Thee in gladness, with body and soul; for Jesus' sake. Amen.

WHAT THIS MEANS TO ME

I owe my very existence to God. Truly, "I am fearfully and wonderfully made" (Ps. 139:14). He made me, soul and body, and gave me my reason and all my senses. These bodily gifts I should diligently care for so that I can use them in a full life of service to Him who gave them.

UNIT 15

THE FIRST ARTICLE — CREATION

God, the Preserver

"I Will Fear No Evil, for Thou Art with Me"

BIBLE STORY

How God Was with Joseph Genesis 50:1-20

Joseph's brothers hated him and sold him as a slave. He was taken to Egypt, where he served for a time in the house of Potiphar, the captain of the king's guards.

God was with Joseph. Potiphar saw that he could trust him and made him caretaker over all his house. Potiphar's wife told wicked lies about Joseph, and he was thrown into prison. Again all seemed lost.

God was still with Joseph, however. With God's help he was able to explain the dreams of the king's butler and baker. When the king also had a dream and no one could explain it, the butler remembered Joseph in prison. He was quickly brought to Pharaoh, the king, and God gave Joseph the wisdom to tell what the king's dream meant.

Pharaoh then made Joseph ruler over all Egypt. Now came seven years of very good crops, and Joseph gathered an abundance of grain and stored it away for safekeeping against the day of famine. Then came seven very bad years. Everywhere people were hungry. Only in Egypt there was food.

One day the brothers of Joseph came down to Egypt to buy grain. He knew them at once; later, when they came a second time, he forgave them the wrong they had done him. "Go back, and get your father and all your families, and bring them to Egypt. I will take care of you," Joseph told them.

So it was that because God watched over Joseph, even the wicked thing his brothers had done to him turned out for the best. Joseph said to his brothers: "Ye thought evil against me, but God meant it unto good."

1. Tell about the evil things that happened to Joseph.

2. Tell about the good things that happened to Joseph.

3. Why could no evil hurt Joseph?

BIBLE READINGS

O Lord, Thou preservest man and beast. Ps. 36:6

The eyes of all wait upon Thee, and Thou givest them their meat in due season. Ps. 145:15

There shall no evil befall thee. Ps. 91:10

I [the Lord] am thy Shield. Gen. 15:1

All things work together for good to them that love God. Rom. 8:28

Oh, give thanks unto the Lord. Ps. 118:1

Serve the Lord with gladness. Ps. 100:2

BIBLE TEACHINGS

God gives life, and only He preserves, or keeps, it. He gives us all that we need for our life: food, and shelter.

God holds off dangers that threaten us and protects us from all evil. Even that which seems evil will turn out for good to them that love God.

God is always our loving Father, although we have done nothing to deserve His love. We may firmly trust God to help us at all times.

Let us all praise God for His goodness and gladly serve Him.

QUESTIONS AND ANSWERS

1. From whom have you received your life?

I have received my life from God, my Creator.

2. How does God preserve your life?

God gives me all things that I need for my life; such as food, clothing, shelter, a sound mind, a healthy body, and strength for my daily tasks.

3. Since all good things are given by God, what should you remember to do?

I should look to God to have all my wants supplied.

4. How does God show Himself to be the Owner of all things and the Ruler of the world?

God uses all things and governs all events according to His will.

5. How does God prevent evil from destroying the world?

By His almighty power God controls the evil that is in the world.

6. Why do you, too, need the power of God's protection?

I am weak and am surrounded by danger and by evil.

7. How does God's loving care preserve your life?

God watches over me and defends me by keeping dangers away.

8. Why does God sometimes permit trials to come to you?

God would lovingly test me and draw me to Himself.

9. How does God protect your life from evil?

God overrules evil and makes it turn out for good.

10. Why have we no right to demand good things from God?

There is no merit or worthiness in us; we are undeserving.

11. Why, then, does God give us many blessings?

God blesses us because He is our loving Father.

12. What should God's fatherly goodness and mercy lead you to do?

I should trust God to help me at all times, and I should be thankful.

13. What should God's loving care remove from your heart?

God's loving care should remove all fear and worry from my heart.

14. Why may you cast all your care on God?

He cares for me.

15. How can you best show your thanks to God for His loving-kindness?

I can best show my thanks to God for His loving-kindness by praising Him and by gladly serving Him with a holy life.

WORD STUDY

abundance: great plenty
to chastise: to punish in order to correct and improve
merit: worth, deserving
to provide: to take care of
to sustain: to support
trial: trouble, hardship
wants: things that are needed

HYMN STANZA

I am Jesus' little lamb,
Ever glad at heart I am;
    For my Shepherd gently guides me,
    Knows my need, and well provides me,
Loves me ev'ry day the same,
Even calls me by my name.

L. H., 648:1

PRAYER

Dear Father in heaven, my life is in the hollow of Thy hand. Grant me grace and wisdom to see that Thy loving-kindness has given me all that I need for my body and life and has kept me from all harm and danger. Open my mouth to sing Thy praise for all Thy Fatherly goodness and mercy; in Jesus' name. Amen.

WHAT THIS MEANS TO ME

I know that the same loving God who made me will watch over me through all my life. His loving, watchful eye will let no evil come near me. He will turn all evil to good if I but love Him. For all this undeserved goodness I ought to praise and serve Him. How foolish I would be if I did not at all times place my trust in God, my mighty Fortress!

UNIT 16

THE SECOND ARTICLE — REDEMPTION

Jesus Christ, the God-Man

"God So Loved the World that He Gave His Only-Begotten Son"

I believe in Jesus Christ, His only Son, our Lord,
who was conceived by the Holy Ghost,
born of the Virgin Mary,
suffered under Pontius Pilate,
was crucified, dead, and buried;
He descended into hell;
the third day He rose again from the dead;
He ascended into heaven,
and sitteth on the right hand of God the Father Almighty;
from thence He shall come to judge the quick and the dead.

What does this mean?

I believe that Jesus Christ,
true God, begotten of the Father from eternity, and also
true man, born of the Virgin Mary,
is my Lord,

who has redeemed me, a lost and condemned creature,

purchased and won me from all sins, from death, and from the power of the devil;

not with gold or silver, but with His holy, precious blood

and with His innocent suffering and death,

that I may be His own, and live under Him in His kingdom, and serve Him in everlasting righteousness, innocence, and blessedness,

even as He is risen from the dead, lives and reigns to all eternity.

This is most certainly true.

BIBLE STORY

The Birth of Jesus

Luke 2:1-14

The little town of Bethlehem was crowded with visitors from far and near. Mighty Caesar Augustus, who ruled over all the world, commanded all the people to have their names put on tax lists in the town of their forefathers. Therefore all the descendants of David went to the city of David, which is called Bethlehem.

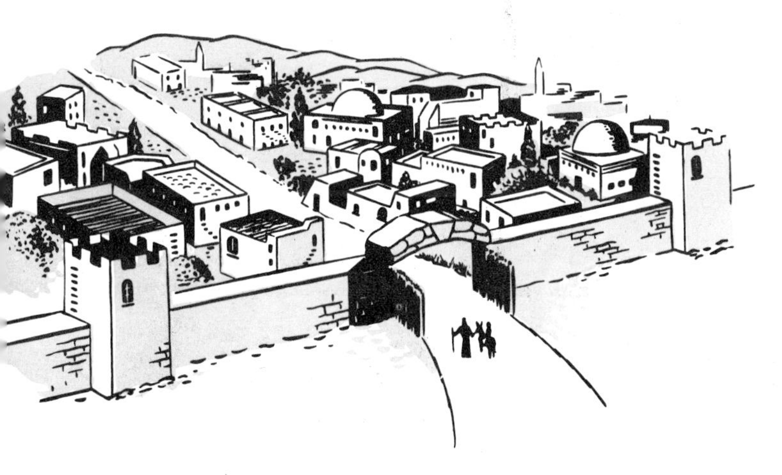

Among them was Joseph, a poor carpenter from Nazareth. He came with Mary, his wife. Every room in the inn was taken, and there was no place left for them but the stable. Here they made themselves comfortable on the straw, as best they could.

That night, in the stable, a son was born to Mary. There was no cradle, and there were no warm blankets. Therefore Mary wrapped her baby in swaddling clothes and laid him in a manger. It was the most wonderful baby ever born, for that son of Mary was at the same time the Son of God, the Savior Jesus Christ.

While this was happening, a radiant angel of God came suddenly to a few frightened shepherds out on the field and told them: "Fear not; for, behold, I bring you good tidings of great joy, which shall be to all people. For unto you is born this day in the city of David a *Savior,* which is *Christ the Lord.* And this shall be a sign unto you: Ye shall find the Babe wrapped in swaddling clothes, lying in a manger."

Suddenly there was with the angel a multitude of the heavenly host, praising God and saying: "Glory to God in the highest, and on earth peace, good will toward men."

1. What brought Joseph and Mary to Bethlehem?
2. Why could they find no room in the inn?
3. Who was the wonderful Baby born to Mary in the stable?
4. Why did He come into this world?
5. What good news did the angel give the shepherds?

BIBLE READINGS

Neither is there salvation in any other; for there is none other name under heaven given among men, whereby we must be saved. Acts 4:12

Thou shalt call His name Jesus; for He shall save His people from their sins. Matt. 1:21

God anointed Jesus of Nazareth with the Holy Ghost and with power. Acts 10:38

This [Jesus Christ] is the true God and eternal Life. 1 John 5:20

There is one God, and one Mediator between God and men, the Man Christ Jesus. 1 Tim. 2:5

BIBLE TEACHINGS

"I believe in Jesus Christ, His only Son, our Lord." These words take us into the very heart of our Christian faith; all that we are and hope to be we owe to Jesus.

Jesus means Savior. He deserves that name, for He is our Savior; He saved us from sin and hell. He is also called Christ, or the Messiah, because God anointed Him with the Holy Ghost to be our Savior.

Jesus Christ is true God, equal with the Father. He proved this by His mighty works, or miracles. Our Savior is also true man, born of the Virgin Mary. He is both true God and true man. For that reason we rightly call Him the God-Man.

QUESTIONS AND ANSWERS

1. In which words do we state the chief teaching of our Christian faith?

In the words, "I believe in Jesus Christ, His only Son, our Lord."

2. Why did God choose the name Jesus for His Son, the Babe of Bethlehem?

The name Jesus tells us that He is the Savior.

3. Why does Jesus mean so much to you?

Jesus means so much to me because He has saved me from hell to heaven, from death to life, from selfishness to love, from sin to service.

4. What does the title "Christ" tell us about Jesus?

It tells us that Jesus was anointed to be our Prophet, Priest, and King.

5. Who is Jesus Christ?

Jesus Christ is the eternal Son of God, who took on human flesh.

6. Why is none other like unto Jesus?

Jesus is true God and true man.

7. Why do you believe that Jesus Christ is true God?

He was begotten of the Father from eternity.

8. Why do you believe that Jesus Christ is true man?

He was born of the Virgin Mary.

9. Why should all men know Jesus and believe in Him?

"There is none other name under heaven given among men whereby we must be saved."

10. What confession are you happy to make now that you know Jesus and believe in Him?

I love Him as my Savior and follow Him as my Lord.

WORD STUDY

to anoint: to put oil upon, to put into office
Mediator: the Go-between
miracle: a wonderful happening beyond the laws of nature
multitude: a great number
to reconcile: to make friends again
tidings: news
swaddling clothes: clothes wrapped round an infant

HYMN STANZA

Hark! the herald angels sing,
"Glory to the newborn King;
  Peace on earth and mercy mild,
  God and sinners reconciled!"
Joyful, all ye nations, rise,
Join the triumph of the skies;
  With th' angelic host proclaim:
  "Christ is born in Bethlehem!"
Hark! the herald angels sing,
"Glory to the newborn King!"

L. H., 94:1

PRAYER

Dear heavenly Father, I thank Thee that by Thy love I have come to know Jesus as my Savior. Grant me grace that I may trust in Him alone and worship Him as my only Redeemer. For His sake hear my prayer. Amen.

WHAT THIS MEANS TO ME

With my whole heart I must believe that Jesus Christ, my Savior, is true God and true man. I must ever believe that this Jesus, God's only-begotten Son, though equal with God the Father, also lived on earth as a true man. Never dare I doubt that Jesus was and is both God and man, for to do so is to deny my faith.

UNIT 17

THE SECOND ARTICLE — REDEMPTION

The Suffering of the God-Man

"Behold the Lamb of God, Which Taketh Away the Sin of the World"

BIBLE STORY

"It Is Finished!"

John 18 and 19

Jesus, the pure and holy Son of God, never sinned. He kept all the Commandments of God perfectly. His heavenly Father said of Him: "This is My beloved Son, in whom I am well pleased."

Yet Jesus let Himself be taken prisoner by His enemies. He let them accuse Him of being a wicked criminal, and He permitted Pontius Pilate, the governor, to give the order to nail Him to a cross, like an evildoer.

When Jesus hung upon the Cross, He suffered the most horrible tortures that can be imagined. His enemies cursed Him; the thieves who were crucified with Him mocked Him; and His friends left Him.

Yes, even God the heavenly Father turned away from Him, and Jesus cried: "My God, My God, why hast Thou forsaken Me?" Jesus suffered all the pains and punishment of hell.

But then it was all over, and Jesus shouted this word of victory: "It is finished!"

His suffering was ended. When He died, His wonderful work of redemption was finished.

He had done all that was needed to be the Savior of the world. He had taken away the sins of all people. "It is finished!"

1. How did the enemies of Jesus torture Him?

2. For what purpose did Jesus suffer and die?

3. Tell what Jesus meant when He said: "It is finished!"

4. What does the death of Christ mean to you?

BIBLE READINGS

No man taketh My life from Me, but I lay it down of Myself. John 10:18

God hath made Him to be sin for us who knew no sin, that we might be made the righteousness of God in Him. 2 Cor. 5:21

Christ died for our sins. 1 Cor. 15:3

Ye were not redeemed with corruptible things, as silver and gold . . . but with the precious blood of Christ, as of a Lamb without blemish and without spot. 1 Peter 1:18, 19

Christ died for all. 2 Cor. 5:15

BIBLE TEACHINGS

Jesus Christ, true God and true man, is my Lord and Savior. He kept the Commandments for me. He suffered under Pontius Pilate and was crucified. This shameful death He suffered, not because He *had* to, but because He *wanted* to.

The sinless Son of God took our sins upon Himself and suffered our punishment. He shed His holy blood to make us holy and righteous before God.

By His holy life and by His innocent suffering and death Jesus saved me. And what He did for me, He did for *all.*

QUESTIONS AND ANSWERS

1. Why do you love Jesus?

I love Jesus because He is my Savior.

2. What did Jesus do to be your Savior?

Jesus kept the Commandments for me, and He suffered and died for me.

3. Why did Jesus suffer and die?

Jesus suffered and died because of His great love for me and all other people.

4. What precious gift have you received through the love of Jesus?

Jesus has given me freedom from sin, death, and the devil.

5. How did Jesus win your freedom?

Jesus presented Himself to His Father as an Offering, a Sacrifice, for my sins.

6. By which act did Jesus offer Himself to His Father?

Jesus took my place in keeping the Law and in suffering the punishment for my sins.

7. What was the price Jesus paid to set you free from evil?

The price Jesus paid was His holy, precious blood.

8. Why is the blood of Jesus accepted by God as an offering for your sins?

It is the precious blood of the sinless One.

9. How did Jesus show that He wants all men to be saved?

"He died for all."

10. How can the blood of Jesus save the whole world?

It is the blood of the Son of God.

11. How does God regard all who trust in the blood of Jesus?

He regards them as holy and righteous.

12. What comforting knowledge does the story of Jesus give you?

I know that Jesus lived and died for me and that now I am a child of God and an heir of salvation.

WORD STUDY

blemish: fault, spot, stain
corruptible: not lasting
infinite: endless
innocent: doing no evil
redemption: deliverance from sin and eternal death
sacrifice: an offering to God

HYMN STANZAS

My faith looks up to Thee,
Thou Lamb of Calvary,
Savior divine.
Now hear me while I pray;
Take all my guilt away;
Oh, let me from this day
Be wholly Thine!

May Thy rich grace impart
Strength to my fainting heart,
My zeal inspire!
As Thou hast died for me,
Oh, may my love to Thee
Pure, warm, and changeless be,
A living fire!

L. H., 394:1, 2

PRAYER

My gracious Lord and Savior, who hast given Thyself as a sacrifice for all men, I thank Thee for Thy unspeakable love, and, I pray Thee, wash me in Thy precious blood from my sins, and make me holy and righteous before God. Amen.

WHAT THIS MEANS TO ME

"Greater love hath no man than this, that a man lay down his life for his friends" (John 15:13). Jesus laid down His life for *me* when He suffered the punishment which *I* deserved because of my sins. This He did because He loved me. May I ever hold before my eyes the Cross, which reminds me of the suffering which God's sinless Son bore to make me holy and righteous before God!

UNIT 18

THE SECOND ARTICLE — REDEMPTION

The Redeeming Death of Jesus

"By His Stripes We Are Healed"

BIBLE STORY

Jesus and the Dying Thief Luke 23:32-43

Not far from Jerusalem, at a place called Calvary, there stood three crosses. Here the soldiers of Pontius Pilate had crucified Jesus and two thieves, one to the right and the other to the left.

As people walked by, they laughed at Jesus and shook their heads. "He saved others," they cried; "Himself He cannot save." Even the two thieves spoke evil against the Lord.

But by and by one of the thieves no longer mocked Jesus. He said to the other thief: "Do you not fear God? This Man has done no wrong, but we are getting what we deserve." Then turning to Jesus, he prayed: "Lord, remember me when Thou comest into Thy kingdom."

And Jesus, His heart full of love, said to the dying thief: "Verily I say unto thee, Today shalt thou be with Me in Paradise."

Several hours later the thief died and went to heaven with Jesus, because he believed that Jesus was suffering and dying for him.

1. **Who was crucified with Jesus?**
2. **How did they at first act toward Jesus?**
3. **Tell about the change in one of them.**
4. **What does Jesus promise to all who die in faith?**

BIBLE READINGS

Behold the Lamb of God, which taketh away the sin of the world. John 1:29

The blood of Jesus Christ, His Son, cleanseth us from all sin. 1 John 1:7

Christ hath abolished death and hath brought life and immortality to light. 2 Tim. 1:10

For this purpose the Son of God was manifested, that He might destroy the works of the devil. 1 John 3:8

Thou wast slain and hast redeemed us to God by Thy blood. Rev. 5:9

Ye are not your own. 1 Cor. 6:19

Where I am, there shall also My servant be. John 12:26

BIBLE TEACHINGS

What we buy and pay for belongs to us. Christ has bought us with His holy, precious blood and with His innocent suffering and death. Therefore we now belong to Him. He is our rightful Lord.

Sin has lost its power because Jesus suffered the punishment for it. Death has lost its sting because Christ died for us. What we call death is only a peaceful sleep for the Christian. Satan cannot claim us as his own, because Jesus has taken away our sin.

We are the free children of God, saved to serve our Savior with thankful hearts and to enjoy the glory of heaven with Him when we die.

QUESTIONS AND ANSWERS

1. Why do you rightfully belong to Jesus?

Jesus has bought me with a price and made me His own.

2. What was the price that Jesus paid to redeem you?

His holy precious blood and His innocent suffering and death.

3. From what has Jesus redeemed you?

Jesus has redeemed me from all sins, from death, and from the power of the devil.

4. For what purpose has Jesus redeemed you?

Jesus has redeemed me, that I might be His own, and live under Him in His kingdom, and serve Him.

5. Why should you gladly serve Jesus?

Jesus is kind and good; He is my Deliverer.

6. Why is it foolish to serve the devil and the world?

The devil and the world are cruel and deceitful; they will separate me from my Savior.

7. Why is it wrong to live for yourself only?

A selfish life is not Christlike; Jesus gave His all for me, and I should live unto Him.

8. How can you render loving service to Christ?

I can do so by worshiping Him and, for His sake, serving my fellow men.

WORD STUDY

to abolish: to do away with
to crucify: to nail to a cross
deceitful: tricky, misleading
immortality: endless life, living forever
to manifest: to make known

HYMN STANZA

Chief of sinners though I be,
Jesus shed His blood for me;
Died that I might live on high,
Lived that I might never die.
As the branch is to the vine,
I am His, and He is mine.

L. H., 342:1

PRAYER

I thank Thee, Lord Jesus, that Thou hast redeemed me and made me Thine own. I give myself to Thee. Help me to love Thee more and more; take me into Thy holy keeping and never, never let me go. Amen.

WHAT THIS MEANS TO ME

With Jesus as my Savior I have nothing to fear. His holy, precious blood has freed me from the guilt of sin, the terror of death, and the murderous power of the devil. Now I am God's own child, and I can live eternally in His heavenly mansions when I die.

UNIT 19

THE SECOND ARTICLE — REDEMPTION

The Resurrection, Ascension, and Session of Jesus

"Thanks Be to God Which Giveth Us the Victory Through Our Lord Jesus Christ"

BIBLE STORY

How Jesus Rose from the Dead and Went Up to Heaven John 21:1-25; Mark 16:1-20

Jesus died on the Cross on Friday afternoon. His beloved friends took Him down from the Cross and laid Him in a grave near by.

Now, early on Sunday morning, just as the sun was rising, some of the women who were friends of Jesus walked sadly toward the grave to anoint the body of Jesus with sweet spices. "Who will move the big stone away from the opening of the grave?" asked the women.

But look! The stone was already rolled away. The women hurried to the grave and found – not Jesus, but an angel clothed in a snow-white garment. Where was Jesus? The women were filled with fear.

The angel said: "Fear not. You are looking for Jesus of Nazareth, who was crucified. *He is risen!* Go, tell His disciples, and especially Peter!"

During the next forty days Jesus often showed Himself alive to His friends. Then He took them to a mountain near Jerusalem. He said to them: "Go ye into all the world, and preach the Gospel to every creature. He that believeth and is baptized shall be saved; but he that believeth not shall be damned."

And even as He was talking with them, He began to ascend. Higher and higher He went until a cloud hid Him and His disciples could see Him no longer. Jesus had gone up into heaven.

1. What did the women expect to find at the grave?
2. What did the angel say to them?
3. What happened on the fortieth day after Christ's resurrection?
4. What great command did Jesus give to His disciples?

BIBLE READINGS

Christ rose again the third day according to the Scriptures. 1 Cor. 15:4

Jesus was delivered for our offenses and raised again for our justification. Rom. 4:25

Because I live, ye shall live also. John 14:19

After the Lord had spoken unto His disciples, He was received up into heaven and sat on the right hand of God. Mark 16:19

All power is given unto Me in heaven and in earth. Matt. 28:18

Lo, I am with you alway, even unto the end of the world. Matt. 28:20

BIBLE TEACHINGS

Christ died for our sins, but He did not stay in the grave. On the third day He became alive again and showed Himself to the devils in hell as the Victor.

By rising from the dead Christ proved that He is truly the Son of God and the Savior of the world. And because He rose from the dead, we, too, shall rise.

After showing Himself alive to His disciples for forty days, Jesus went up to heaven to rule over all the world and especially to take care of His believers.

QUESTIONS AND ANSWERS

1. **What great victory did Jesus win on Easter Day?**

   The third day He rose again from the dead.

2. **What does the resurrection of Jesus prove?**

   The resurrection of Jesus proves that Jesus is truly the Son of God and the Savior of the world.

3. **What should we remember when we are sad and discouraged?**

   We should remember that Christ's victory over death and the devil is our own victory.

4. **Which wonderful promise of Jesus will be fulfilled for all believers?**

   "Because I live, ye shall live also."

5. **To whom did Jesus show Himself after the Resurrection?**

   Jesus showed Himself to His friends.

6. **Why did Jesus show Himself to His friends?**

   He wished to strengthen their faith in His resurrection.

7. **Why is Christ's resurrection important?**

   "If Christ be not raised, your faith is vain; ye are yet in your sins."

8. **What happened on the fortieth day after Christ's resurrection?**

   He ascended into heaven.

9. **Where is Jesus now?**

   Jesus is sitting at the right hand of God the Father Almighty and is everywhere.

10. How is Jesus now using His divine power?

Jesus now rules over all the world as the glorious King of Kings.

11. What sweet consolation is there in knowing that Jesus is the King of Kings?

The King is our Savior; He takes special care of His own.

12. Which is the best and happiest life, now and forevermore?

"To live under Him in His kingdom."

WORD STUDY

consolation: comfort
disciple: a pupil, or follower
justification: declaring the sinner not guilty
offense: sin
resurrection: rising from the dead
victor: winner

HYMN STANZAS

I know that my Redeemer lives;
What comfort this sweet sentence gives!
He lives, He lives, who once was dead;
He lives, my everliving Head.

He lives, all glory to His name!
He lives, my Jesus, still the same.
Oh, the sweet joy this sentence gives,
"I know that my Redeemer lives!"

L. H., 200:1,8

PRAYER

Blessed Jesus, who art the Prince of life and the Lord of glory, I adore Thee for Thy victory over death. Be Thou ever near me with Thy living presence. Grant me to believe that by Thy power, I, too, shall rise from the dead. Let me trust in Thy love, and do Thou take me at last to heaven, where I shall see Thee face to face, in heaven's endless day. Amen.

WHAT THIS MEANS TO ME

How happy I am to know that my Jesus rose from the dead, ascended to heaven, yet is ever present, and now rules the world in wisdom and glory! If I die trusting in Jesus, He will raise my body on the Last Day and take it to heaven. He is even now in heaven and on earth, watching over me and all those who trust in Him.

"Christ is ris'n," today we cry;
Now He lives no more to die.' (*L. H.*, 191:4.)

UNIT 20

THE SECOND ARTICLE — REDEMPTION

The Last Judgment

"He Shall Reign Forever and Ever.
King of Kings and Lord of Lords"

BIBLE STORY

How Jesus will Judge All People Matt. 25:31-46

Shortly before His suffering and death Jesus told His disciples that He would come to judge the living and the dead.

How wonderful that will be! On the Last Day of the world Jesus will come in all His glory as the

King of heaven, and all His holy angels will come with Him. Then Jesus will sit on His throne, and all the people then living as well as all the millions that ever lived will stand before Him. You will not be able to count them all.

Jesus will put all the believers on His right hand, and all the unbelievers on the left. "Come, you blessed children of God," King Jesus will say to those on His right, "enter the beautiful home which your heavenly Father has made ready for you. For I was hungry, and you fed Me; thirsty, and you gave Me drink; I was a stranger, and you took Me into your home; naked, and you clothed Me; sick and in prison, and you visited Me."

"But when did we do that? We do not remember at all."

"Every time you were kind to anyone in trouble, you did it for Me," Jesus will say.

How different will be His words to the unbelievers! "I was hungry and thirsty, a stranger and naked, sick and in prison, and you never helped Me. So you must go to the punishment of hell forever."

"But, Lord, we never had a chance to do anything for You!" they will cry.

Jesus will answer: "Every time you had a chance to help someone in trouble and failed to do so, you refused to do it for Me."

1. When will Jesus come back to earth?

2. Why will He come?

3. How do the children of God show that they love Him?

4. How do the unbelievers show that they do not love God?

BIBLE READINGS

This same Jesus, which is taken up from you into heaven, shall so come in like manner as ye have seen Him go into heaven. Acts 1:11

Of that day and that hour knoweth no man . . . but the Father. Mark 13:32

When these things [the signs before the Last Day] begin to come to pass, then look up, and lift up your heads; for your redemption draweth nigh. Luke 21:28

The Son of Man shall come in His glory, and all the holy angels with Him. Matt. 25:31

God will judge the world in righteousness by that Man whom He hath ordained. Acts 17:31

BIBLE TEACHINGS

On the Last Day, which is known only to God, our Savior will come back as the King of Glory to judge all people, the living and the dead.

This will be a terrible day for the wicked, but a most happy day for all children of God. On that day Jesus will send the unbelievers to hell, but He will take the believers to that beautiful home which His heavenly Father made ready for them.

What a wonderful Savior we have! Happy are we if we love and trust in Him.

QUESTIONS AND ANSWERS

1. **When shall we see Jesus?**

   We shall see Jesus on the Last Day of the world and in all eternity.

2. **When will the Last Day come?**

   Only God knows when the Last Day will come, but that day is surely drawing near.

3. **How will Jesus come on the Last Day?**

   Jesus will come in all His glory, and all the holy angels will come with Him.

4. **For what purpose will Jesus come on the Last Day?**

   Jesus will come to judge the quick and the dead.

5. **Why did Jesus not judge the world immediately after His resurrection?**

   Jesus wished to have the Gospel preached in all the world.

6. **Why will Judgment Day be a terrible day for the unbelievers?**

   On that day Jesus will send the unbelievers to their everlasting punishment.

7. **Why will Judgment Day be a day of joy for the believers?**

   On that day Jesus will take the believers to the beautiful home which He and His Father have made ready for them.

8. **To what should the coming of Judgment Day move us?**

   To watchfulness and prayer.

9. **How do we remain watchful?**

   By always doing what Jesus would have us to do.

10. How do we remain ready for the Last Day through prayer?

By asking Jesus to keep us in true faith and love.

11. What ought we to do with special zeal while there is yet time?

We ought to try to win souls for Christ while there is yet time.

WORD STUDY

aye: always, ever
frame: body
Judgment Day: the Last Day
to ordain: to appoint
redemption: deliverance

HYMN STANZA

Lord, on that solemn Day,
    When all the dead are waking,
Stretch o'er my grave Thy hand,
    Thyself my slumbers breaking.
Then let me hear Thy voice,
    Change Thou this earthly frame,
And bid me aye rejoice
    With those who love Thy name.

L. H., 395:8

PRAYER

Blessed Lord Jesus, who at Thy first appearing didst come to save me and at Thy second appearing wilt come to judge me, I pray Thee, make me watchful for Thy coming on the Last Day, that I may be ready to meet Thee as my Lord and King. Come, Lord Jesus; come quickly. Amen.

WHAT THIS MEANS TO ME

I know not when Jesus will come to call me home, but I will so believe and live as to be ready to go with Him at any time. Firmly believing that my sins are washed away in His blood, I will eagerly look forward to that happy day when I shall meet Him face to face. My goal will be to do only those things that please Jesus. I will try not to do anything that I would be ashamed to be doing when Jesus comes to take me home.

UNIT 21

THE THIRD ARTICLE — SANCTIFICATION

The Holy Ghost

"I Will Pour Out My Spirit Upon All Flesh"

I believe in the Holy Ghost;
the holy Christian Church, the communion of saints;
the forgiveness of sins;
the resurrection of the body;
and the life everlasting. Amen.

What does this mean?

I believe that I cannot by my own reason or strength
believe in Jesus Christ, my Lord, or come to Him;
but the Holy Ghost has called me by the Gospel,
enlightened me with His gifts,
sanctified and kept me in the true faith;
even as He calls, gathers, enlightens, and sanctifies
the whole Christian Church on earth, and keeps it
with Jesus Christ in the one true faith;
in which Christian Church He daily and richly forgives all sins to me and all believers,
and will at the Last Day raise up me and all the dead,
and give unto me and all believers in Christ eternal life.
This is most certainly true.

BIBLE STORY

How the Holy Ghost Came Down Upon the Disciples

Acts 2:1-41

"I will send you the Holy Ghost to be your Friend," said Jesus to His disciples a little while before He left them. After Jesus had ascended into heaven, the disciples came together every day in a certain house in Jerusalem, waiting for their Lord's promise to come true.

On the tenth day the sound as of a rushing mighty wind from heaven suddenly filled the whole house where they were. At the same time tongues as of fire could be seen above the heads of all of them. Most surprising of all, the disciples began to preach about the wonderful works of God in many languages they had never known before.

Many people from all parts of the world heard them preach and cried: "What strange thing is happening here? How can these men speak to us in our own language?"

Peter explained it to them: "This is the coming of the Holy Ghost, as God promised long ago." Peter added: "Jesus of Nazareth did many wonderful deeds to prove that He is the Son of God; Him you nailed to the Cross. But He became alive again and went up to heaven to rule over all the world."

The people took Peter's sermon to heart. "What shall we do?" they asked.

Peter said: "Be sorry for your sins, and be baptized in the name of Jesus Christ for the forgiveness of your sins, and you shall receive the gift of faith from the Holy Ghost. This promise is meant for you and for your children."

On that day about three thousand people became believers.

1. **The festival of the Holy Ghost is called Pentecost. Ask your teacher what it means.**
2. **Of what were the sound of the wind and the fiery tongues the sign?**
3. **Who gave the disciples the power to speak in different languages?**
4. **How did the people become Christians?**

BIBLE READINGS

The natural man receiveth not the things of the Spirit of God. 1 Cor. 2:14

No man can say that Jesus is the Lord but by the Holy Ghost. 1 Cor. 12:3

Turn Thou me, and I shall be turned. Jer. 31:18

Come unto Me, all ye that labor and are heavy laden, and I will give you rest. Matt. 11:28

God hath shined in our hearts. 2 Cor. 4:6

God called you by our Gospel. 2 Thess. 2:14

Faith cometh by hearing. Rom. 10:17

We are God's workmanship, created in Christ Jesus unto good works. Eph. 2:10

Ye are kept by the power of God through faith unto salvation. 1 Peter 1:5

BIBLE TEACHINGS

The inspired Apostle Paul once wrote: "No man can say that Jesus is the Lord but by the Holy Ghost." Without the Holy Ghost, therefore, we are helpless; we can understand nothing about Jesus Christ, our Savior; we can do nothing to believe in Him and be saved.

By nature our heart is filled with unbelief and hatred toward God.

Only the Holy Ghost, who is true God with the Father and the Son, can change our heart. He invites and urges us to come to Jesus; He makes us able to know and to believe in Jesus as our Savior. He gives us power to live as God wants us to live. He also keeps us in the faith to the end. In a word: The Holy Ghost *sanctifies* us – makes us holy before God through faith in Christ.

The Holy Ghost does all His wonderful work through the Gospel. The Gospel is the power of God unto salvation to everyone that believes.

QUESTIONS AND ANSWERS

1. **What does St. Paul mean when he says: "No man can say that Jesus is the Lord but by the Holy Ghost"?**

   Only the Holy Ghost can enable a person to believe that Jesus is Savior and Lord.

2. **Why can we not believe in Jesus by our own reason or strength?**

   In spiritual matters we are blind and dead and opposed to God.

3. **How does the Holy Ghost bring us to faith in Jesus?**

   The Holy Ghost persuades us that Jesus Christ loves us and that He died for us.

4. **Where is the story of Christ's love to be found?**

   The story of Christ's love is to be found in the Gospel of Jesus Christ.

5. **How does the Holy Ghost use the Gospel of Jesus Christ?**

   By means of the Gospel of Jesus Christ the Holy Ghost invites, or calls, us to believe in Jesus.

6. **Why is the Gospel called the power of God unto salvation?**

   Through the Gospel the Holy Ghost makes us able and willing to believe in Jesus and to love Him.

7. **What great miracle does the Holy Ghost work in you through the Gospel of Jesus Christ?**

   Through the Gospel the Holy Ghost changes my heart and enlightens my mind, so that I see and love Jesus as my personal Savior.

8. **What marvelous changes has the Word of the Gospel brought about in you?**

   I was dead, but now I live; I was blind, but now I see; I was helpless, but now I am strengthened; I hated God and man, but now love dwells in my heart.

9. For what other purpose does the Holy Ghost use the Gospel?

The Holy Ghost gives me power to lead a godly life and keeps me in the true faith until my end.

10. Why is the Gospel God's most precious gift to you?

The Gospel gives me faith in Christ and thus makes me holy before God.

WORD STUDY

communion of saints: all people who believe in Jesus Christ
Pentecost: the fiftieth day after Easter
to persuade: to cause someone to believe
to reveal: to make known
to sanctify: to make holy
God's workmanship: what God has made

HYMN STANZAS

Come, Holy Spirit, come!
Let Thy bright beams arise;
Dispel the sorrow from our minds,
The darkness from our eyes.

Convince us of our sin,
Then lead to Jesus' blood.
And to our wond'ring view reveal
The mercies of our God.

L. H., 225:1, 4

PRAYER

O Holy Spirit, who makest known the deep things of God, I thank Thee that Thou hast led me to know Jesus as my Savior. Help me to show my faith by a holy life, and keep me in Thy truth unto my life's end; for Jesus' sake. Amen.

WHAT THIS MEANS TO ME

What Jesus has done for me I could never believe if God's Holy Spirit had not called me by the Gospel and led me to know and love my dear Savior. How thankful I ought be that God has sent His Holy Spirit to bring me to the loving arms of Jesus! Realizing this, I ought to pray God daily to keep His Holy Spirit ever abiding in my heart, sanctifying my life and keeping me in the true faith unto my end.

UNIT 22

THE THIRD ARTICLE — SANCTIFICATION

The Holy Christian Church

"Christ Loved the Church and Gave Himself for It"

BIBLE STORY

Christ's Promise to Build His Church Matt. 16:13-20

Our Lord Jesus spoke many wonderful words and did many wonderful deeds. Everybody who heard or saw Him had certain ideas about Him.

One day, when Jesus was alone with His disciples, He asked them: "Who do men say that I, the Son of Man, am?"

They said to Him: "Some say that Thou art John the Baptist; some, that Thou art Elijah; and others, that Thou art Jeremiah, or some great prophet who has come back to earth."

"But who do you say that I am?" Jesus then asked.

Simon Peter, speaking for all the disciples, answered: "Thou art the Christ, the Son of the living God!"

This fine and true answer pleased Jesus. He said to Peter: "You are Peter, and upon this rock [the truth which you confessed] I will build My Church; and the gates of hell [all the powers of the devil] shall not prevail against it."

1. **Repeat the words which Peter said to Jesus.**
2. **What is Jesus building on this truth?**
3. **What did Jesus promise to His Church?**

BIBLE READINGS

Upon this rock I will build My Church; and the gates of hell shall not prevail against it. Matt. 16:18

The Lord knoweth them that are His. 2 Tim. 2:19

Other foundation can no man lay than that is laid, which is Jesus Christ. 1 Cor. 3:11

Ye are fellow citizens with the saints and of the household of God. Eph. 2:19

BIBLE TEACHINGS

All true believers in Christ are brothers and sisters in the family of God. We call this family the holy Christian Church, or the communion of saints.

The Church is also likened to a building, of which Christ is the Foundation. The Church is also called a body, of which Christ is the Head.

The Church is holy, because all its members are saints in God's sight, cleansed of all their sins by the blood of Christ.

Only God knows who the members of His Church are, because He alone can look into men's hearts and see whether they believe.

To be and to remain a member of the holy Christian Church, of God's holy family, should be my strongest wish, because then I share in all the blessings which God gives to His children.

Furthermore, I shall join a congregation which preaches the Word of God in its truth and purity, and I shall support it with my prayers, time, talents, and money.

QUESTIONS AND ANSWERS

1. Who are God's holy people?

All true believers in Christ are God's holy people.

2. How are all believers in Christ related to one another?

All believers in Christ are brothers and sisters in the family of God.

3. By what name do we know the family of God?

We know the family of God as the holy Christian Church, or the communion of saints.

4. Why is the Church called the communion of saints?

The members are cleansed of all their sins by the blood of Christ.

5. Why should no one in the Church think himself better than others?

All are sinners and are cleansed by the same blood.

6. Who is the Head of the Church?

"One is your Master, even Christ; and all ye are brethren."

7. Why should you wish, most of all, to be a member of God's holy family?

As a member of God's holy family I share in all the blessings which God gives to His children.

8. How do you become a member of the holy Christian Church?

I become a member of the holy Christian Church through faith in Jesus Christ.

9. What should prompt you to unite with other Christians in a congregation?

The desire to learn more of Jesus and to proclaim His Word to others.

10. Which Christian congregation should you join?

I should join only such a congregation as teaches the Word of God in its truth and purity and administers the Sacraments correctly.

11. How will you thank God that He has made you a member of the holy Christian Church?

I will support the work of the Church with my prayers, time, talents, and money.

WORD STUDY

foundation: that part on which a building stands
loyal: true, faithful
to prevail: to gain the victory
to proclaim: to make known
talent: ability
unity: being joined together in one body

HYMN STANZA

The Church's one Foundation
   Is Jesus Christ, her Lord;
She is His new creation
   By water and the Word.
From heaven He came and sought her
   To be His holy bride;
With His own blood He bought her,
   And for her life He died.

L. H., 473:1

PRAYER

Father in heaven, who through the Holy Ghost hast gathered all believers together and made them one in Thy Church, grant unto me and my fellow believers a strong faith, that I may ever remain with them in the unity of the spirit and, together with all Thy holy people, share in Thy blessings to the Church; through Jesus Christ, the Lord and Head of the Church. Amen.

WHAT THIS MEANS TO ME

What a blessed privilege it is to be a member of God's holy family, the holy Christian Church, and thus share in all the blessings which God gives to His children! If I truly appreciate this great blessing, I will earnestly try to bring the saving Gospel message of Christ to others who know not of His love. I know that God's holy family will rejoice if through my missionary zeal one more child is led to His waiting arms.

UNIT 23

THE THIRD ARTICLE — SANCTIFICATION

The Forgiveness of Sins

"To The Lord, Our God, Belong Mercies and Forgivenesses"

BIBLE STORY

God's Greatest Gift to His Church Mark 2:1-12

The city of Capernaum on the northwest shore of the Sea of Galilee was the favorite city of the Lord Jesus. He often came here and spent much time in preaching and in healing the sick.

Once again Jesus had come to Capernaum. The people soon heard of it and hurried to the house where Jesus was staying. They came to hear and to see Him. "Perhaps He will do another wonderful deed," they thought.

Soon the house was crowded to the doors. No one could get into the house any more. But outside there was a group of men who wanted to get to Jesus. They were carrying a friend on a bed. He was very sick. He could not move his arms or legs, and he suffered terrible pains. His friends knew that Jesus could help.

When they saw that they could not get through the door, they carried the bed up to the flat roof of the house. There they opened part of the roof and lowered their sick friend through the opening, until he was right in front of Jesus.

Jesus loved the men for their strong faith in Him. He saw how greatly the sick man was suffering, and He was willing to make him well. But first Jesus said: "Son, be of good cheer. Your sins are forgiven." Only then did Jesus heal the man's sick body. Jesus knew that sin is the greatest trouble of all and that forgiveness of sin is the most wonderful blessing. It is the greatest gift which He could give.

1. **What did the people of Capernaum do when they heard that Jesus was in the city?**
2. **What brought one group of men to the house where Jesus was?**
3. **How did they get their sick friend to Jesus?**
4. **The forgiveness of sins is God's greatest gift to men. How did Jesus show this to be true?**
5. **Which is easier: to forgive sins or to heal sickness?**

BIBLE READINGS

Bless the Lord, O my soul, and forget not all His benefits; who forgiveth all thine iniquities.
Ps. 103:2, 3

In Jesus Christ we have redemption through His blood, the forgiveness of sins, according to the riches of His grace. Eph. 1:7

There is forgiveness with Thee. Ps. 130:4

By grace are ye saved through faith; and that not of yourselves; it is the gift of God. Eph. 2:8

What must I do to be saved? Believe on the Lord Jesus Christ, and thou shalt be saved.
Acts 16:30, 31

Son, be of good cheer; thy sins be forgiven thee.
Matt. 9:2

BIBLE TEACHINGS

The happiest people on earth are the members of God's family. In the Christian Church, God gives me the one thing which I need most and which alone can make me happy: the forgiveness of sins.

Even though I am a child of God and love my Savior, I still sin daily. Therefore I daily need forgiveness of my sin in order to remain God's child.

God gives me what I need. Daily and richly He forgives me all my sins, as He has promised in His Word: "I will remember thy sins no more."

I can do nothing to earn the forgiveness of sins. Christ, my Savior, has already earned it for me. Now

God grants me forgiveness as a free gift. I need only believe God's promise with all my heart. Therefore I rejoice to say: "I am saved by grace."

QUESTIONS AND ANSWERS

1. **Why is the forgiveness of sins the greatest blessing in the world?**

   The forgiveness of sins brings us into God's family as His children.

2. **Why do even Christians need forgiveness of sins?**

   Christians need forgiveness of sins because they sin every day.

3. **Why cannot our good works earn forgiveness of sins?**

   "All our righteousnesses are as filthy rags."

4. **Who alone has earned forgiveness of sins for us?**

   Christ, our Savior, has earned forgiveness of sins for us.

5. **Through what means does God offer forgiveness as a free gift?**

   Through the Gospel of Jesus Christ God offers forgiveness as a free gift.

6. **When do we receive the forgiveness which God offers?**

   We receive forgiveness when with all our heart we believe God's promise: "I will remember thy sins no more."

7. **How do we become willing and able to believe God's promise?**

   The Holy Ghost fills our heart with desire and strength to believe the promise of God.

8. **How should God's forgiveness make us feel?**

   It should make us feel humble, thankful, and full of joy.

9. **Why has no Christian a right to be boastful and proud?**

   Every Christian must confess: "I am saved by grace alone."

10. **Why need a Christian never despair?**

    God daily and richly forgives all sins to all believers.

11. **How may you show your thankfulness for the grace of God?**

    "I will sing of the mercies of the Lord forever."

12. **Why do we desire to share the Gospel with the heathen?**

    "To turn them from darkness to light, that they may receive forgiveness of sins."

WORD STUDY

crimson: deep red color, almost like purple
to despair: to lose hope
grace: undeserved kindness
iniquities: sins
penitent: sorry for having done wrong

HYMN STANZA

I lay my sins on Jesus,
The spotless Lamb of God;
He bears them all and frees us
From the accursed load.

I bring my guilt to Jesus
To wash my crimson stains
White in His blood most precious
Till not a spot remains.

L. H., 652:1

PRAYER

My dear God and Father, I am not worthy to be called Thy child, because I sin daily in thought, word, and deed. For Jesus' sake forgive me all my sins. Let me trust in Thy grace and be forever Thine. Amen.

WHAT THIS MEANS TO ME

I daily sin much. I ought seriously to try to avoid sin and walk closer with Jesus. But my sins will still be with me every day. How thankful I ought to be that as a child in God's holy Family I receive full and complete forgiveness for all sins every day! This great gift I receive through faith in Jesus from my ever-forgiving Father in heaven.

UNIT 24

THE THIRD ARTICLE — SANCTIFICATION

The Resurrection of the Body, and the Life Everlasting

"In My Father's House Are Many Mansions"

BIBLE STORY

The Rich Man and Poor Lazarus Luke 16:19-31

A certain rich man lived in a large, beautiful home. He wore the finest, most expensive clothes. With his friends he enjoyed the most tasty foods every day. He had everything that money could buy, and he used it for his own pleasure.

At the same time a poor, sick beggar named Lazarus lay in the street outside the rich man's door. He hoped to get a few crumbs from the rich man's table. His whole body was covered with painful sores. But the rich man did not help Lazarus. Only the dogs came and licked his sores.

One day Lazarus was gone. He had died, and the holy angels had carried him into heaven, the beautiful home of the blessed people of God.

The rich man also died and was buried. But he went to hell.

1. Tell about the difference between the rich man and Lazarus in this life.
2. Where did Lazarus find his true home?
3. What became of the rich man?
4. Why did these two arrive at two different places?

BIBLE READINGS

The hour is coming in the which all that are in the graves shall hear His voice and shall come forth; they that have done good, unto the resurrection of life; and they that have done evil, unto the resurrection of damnation. John 5:28, 29

Christ shall change our vile body that it may be fashioned like unto His glorious body. Phil. 3:21

In Thy presence is fullness of joy; at Thy right hand there are pleasures forevermore. Ps. 16:11

Verily I say unto thee, Today shalt thou be with Me in Paradise. Luke 23:43

I have a desire to depart and to be with Christ, which is far better. Phil. 1:23

BIBLE TEACHINGS

This world will someday come to an end. On that day God will make all dead people alive again. The unbelievers will be sent to everlasting pains in hell, but the believers will rise to everlasting life in heaven. Heaven is the true home of God's people.

The believers will have the same body they had on earth, but it will be perfect, free from all sin, pain, and death. With body and soul united again, they will be with Christ in joy and glory without end.

Lovingly my Savior will welcome me and all believers with the words: "Come, ye blessed of My Father, inherit the kingdom prepared for you from the foundation of the world."

I believe this with all my heart because God's promises are sure.

QUESTIONS AND ANSWERS

1. **Why do we believe in the resurrection of the body?**

   God has promised to raise our bodies. His promise is sure, for "with God all things are possible."

2. **What body will the believers have in heaven?**

   The believers will have the same body they had on earth.

3. **How will their bodies be different in heaven from what they were on earth?**

   In heaven their bodies will be perfect; they will be free from all sin, pain, and death.

4. **Whose body will our resurrection body resemble?**

   Our resurrection body will be fashioned like unto Christ's glorious body.

5. What difference will there be in the resurrection of the dead?

The believers will rise with glorified bodies to everlasting life in heaven; the unbelievers will rise to everlasting damnation.

6. What does it mean to be in heaven?

To be in heaven means to be with Christ forevermore.

7. What will be the greatest joy in heaven?

"We shall see Him as He is."

8. Why are you sure that you will see God face to face?

God is faithful; all His promises are sure.

9. Why are you especially thankful to God the Holy Ghost?

It is God the Holy Ghost who has created and preserved in me the faith through which I obtain eternal life.

10. How do we show that we regard heaven as our true home?

By setting our hearts on things above, and not on things of the earth.

11. Why should our heart evermore be fixed on God?

The Bible says of God: "With Thee is the fountain of life; in Thy light shall we see light."

WORD STUDY

Dayspring: beginning of day (used of Jesus)
to fashion: to make
to inherit: to receive as a gift from one's father
Paradise: heaven
resurrection: rising from the dead
summons: call
vile: unclean, very bad

HYMN STANZA

Ah, thou Dayspring from on high,
  Grant that at Thy next appearing
We who in the graves do lie
  May arise, Thy summons hearing,
And rejoice in our new life,
  Far from strife.

L. H., 539:4

PRAYER

Lord Jesus Christ, who hast gone to prepare a place for us, help us by Thy Holy Spirit to remain steadfast in the true faith unto our end and hereafter to dwell with Thee in Paradise. Amen.

WHAT THIS MEANS TO ME

Confidently believing the sure promise of God, I need have no fear of death and the grave. I know that when I die, I will be only asleep in Jesus. On Judgment Day He will awaken my body and join it with my soul in the mansions above. There I will live eternally in the presence of the Holy Trinity.

UNIT 25

THE INTRODUCTION

Prayer in General

"Lord, Teach Us to Pray"

Our Father who art in heaven. Hallowed be Thy name. Thy kingdom come. Thy will be done on earth as it is in heaven. Give us this day our daily bread. And forgive us our trespasses, as we forgive those who trespass against us. And lead us not into temptation, but deliver us from evil. For Thine is the kingdom and the power and the glory forever and ever. Amen.

THE INTRODUCTION

Our Father who art in heaven.

What does this mean?

God would by these words tenderly invite us to believe that He is our true Father, and that we are His true children, so that we may with all boldness and confidence ask Him as dear children ask their dear father.

BIBLE STORY

Abraham's Prayer for Sodom Genesis 18:16-33

Not far from the home of Abraham was the city of Sodom, where his nephew Lot lived. The people of Sodom were very wicked and ungodly.

One day the Lord God visited Abraham and told him that He would destroy Sodom. Abraham at once thought of Lot and asked God: "Wilt Thou destroy the good with the wicked? Perhaps there are fifty righteous people in Sodom."

"If I find fifty righteous there, I will spare all the people," said the Lord.

"I have no right to speak to Thee, Lord," continued Abraham, "but wilt Thou destroy the city if there are forty-five righteous?"

"No, if there are forty-five righteous in the city, I will not destroy it."

"Perhaps there are forty."

"I will spare the city for the sake of the forty."

"Do not be angry, Lord, if I speak again, but there may be thirty."

"I will not destroy it if I find thirty there."

"But what if there are twenty?"

"I will not destroy it for the twenty's sake."

"O Lord, be not angry if I ask once more. Maybe there are at least ten righteous."

"I will not destroy it for the ten's sake."

Then the Lord went His way, and Abraham returned home.

1. **Why did God intend to destroy Sodom?**
2. **How did Abraham try to change God's intention?**
3. **How often did Abraham ask God to spare Sodom?**
4. **How did God show His willingness to listen to Abraham?**

BIBLE READINGS

Doubtless Thou art our Father. Is. 63:16

Let the words of my mouth and the meditation of my heart be acceptable in Thy sight, O Lord, my Strength and my Redeemer. Ps. 19:14

When ye pray, use not vain repetitions, as the heathen do. Matt. 6:7

I will that men pray everywhere. 1 Tim. 2:8

Pray without ceasing. 1 Thess. 5:17

I exhort that prayers be made for all men. 1 Tim. 2:1

Verily, verily, I say unto you, Whatsoever ye shall ask the Father in My name, He will give it you. John 16:23

Ask, and it shall be given you. Matt. 7:7

Lord, teach us to pray. Luke 11:1

BIBLE TEACHINGS

God is our heavenly Father, and we are His beloved children for Jesus' sake. We may talk with God as children talk freely with their father. Such heart-to-heart talking with God is prayer. Saying the words with the lips only is no prayer.

God wants us to pray everywhere, at all times, and for all people on earth, even for our enemies. We may ask for anything good.

Our heavenly Father has promised to hear us whenever we pray in the name of Jesus and according to His will. If He does not give us what we ask for, He gives us something better.

The best prayer of all is the Lord's Prayer, which the Lord Jesus gave His disciples. Here our Savior Himself teaches us how to pray.

QUESTIONS AND ANSWERS

1. What is a prayer?

A prayer is a heart-to-heart talk with God.

2. Why should we pray often?

We need God's help at all times, especially in times of trouble.

3. Why have we a right to pray to God?

God is our true Father, and we are His true children by faith in Jesus Christ.

4. Where does God want us to pray?

God wants us to pray everywhere, especially when alone in our room, or with our family at home, or with the congregation in the House of God.

5. When does God want us to pray?

God wants us to pray at all times, especially every morning and evening, before and after meals, in trouble and temptation.

6. For whom does God want us to pray?

God wants us to pray for ourselves and all others, for our friends and loved ones, and also for our enemies.

7. For what may we ask God in our prayers?

We may ask God for everything that is to His glory and to our good.

8. Why may we pray with great confidence?

God has promised to hear all prayers that are offered out of a sincere heart, in the name of Jesus, in true faith, and according to His will.

9. What three ways has God of answering prayer?

He says: "Yes," "No," or "Wait."

10. When does God say "yes"?

When what we ask for is good for us.

11. When does God say "no"?

When what we ask for is not good for us.

12. When does God say "wait"?

When what we ask for will be good for us later.

13. Which is the first prayer given to the Christian Church?

The Lord's Prayer is Christ's prayer given to the Christian Church.

14. Why is it called the Lord's Prayer?

The Lord Himself gave it to His disciples and to us.

15. What are three parts of the Lord's Prayer?

The Introduction, the Seven Petitions, and the Conclusion.

16. What is the Introduction?

The Introduction is the opening sentence, in which we speak to God as to our Father.

17. What do we ask of our Father in the first three petitions?

We ask for heavenly blessings.

18. What do we ask of our Father in the Fourth Petition?

We ask for earthly blessings.

19. What do we ask of our Father in the last three petitions?

We ask for deliverance from sin and all evil.

20. How do we conclude the Lord's Prayer?

We say, For Thine is the kingdom and the power and the glory forever and ever. Amen.

21. By what name do we call upon the Triune God in the Lord's Prayer?

We say, "Our Father who art in heaven."

22. Why would God have us address Him as our *Father*?

God would by these words tenderly invite us to believe that He is our true Father and that we are His true children.

23. With what feeling should we pray to God?

We should pray to Him with all boldness and confidence.

24. When do we pray to God with all boldness?

When we pray to Him without fear.

25. When do we pray to God with all confidence?

When we are sure that He will hear and help us.

26. How trustingly should we pray to our Father?

We should ask Him as dear children ask their dear father.

WORD STUDY

ceasing: stopping
confidence: trust
to exhort: to urge
intercession: pleading for another
meditation: quiet thought
to petition: to ask
privilege: a special right
sincere: honest
vain: empty, useless, worthless

HYMN STANZAS

What a Friend we have in Jesus,
All our sins and griefs to bear!
What a privilege, to carry
Everything to God in prayer!
Oh, what peace we often forfeit,
Oh, what needless pain we bear,
All because we do not carry
Everything to God in prayer!

Have we trials and temptations,
Is there trouble anywhere?
We should never be discouraged,
Take it to the Lord in prayer.
Can we find a friend so faithful
Who will all our sorrows share?
Jesus knows our ev'ry weakness, –
Take it to the Lord in prayer.

L. H., 457:1, 2

PRAYER

Dear Father in heaven, who hast told me to pray and hast promised to hear me, lead me by Thy Spirit to make all my wants known to Thee. Give me those gifts which are good for me; through Jesus Christ, my Savior. Amen.

WHAT THIS MEANS TO ME

As a child of God I ought to speak to my heavenly Father freely and often. He has promised to hear and answer me every time I pray in the name of Jesus. If I want the fullness of God's blessing, I ought to "pray without ceasing."

UNIT 26

THE FIRST THREE PETITIONS

Praying for Spiritual Blessings

"Seek Ye First the Kingdom of God"

THE FIRST PETITION

Hallowed be Thy name.

What does this mean?

God's name is indeed holy in itself;
but we pray in this petition
that it may be holy among us also.

How is this done?

[God's name is hallowed]
When the Word of God is taught in its truth and purity,
and we, as the children of God,
also lead a holy life according to it.
This grant us, dear Father in heaven.
But he that teaches and lives otherwise than God's Word teaches,
profanes the name of God among us.
From this preserve us, Heavenly Father.

THE SECOND PETITION

Thy kingdom come.

What does this mean?

The kingdom of God comes indeed without our prayer, of itself;
but we pray in this petition
that it may come unto us also.

How is this done?

[The Kingdom of God comes to us]
When our heavenly Father gives us His Holy Spirit,
so that by His grace we believe His holy Word and
lead a godly life, here in time and hereafter in eternity.

THE THIRD PETITION

Thy will be done on earth as it is in heaven.

What does this mean?

The good and gracious will of God is done indeed without our prayer;
but we pray in this petition
that it may be done among us also.

How is this done?

[God's good and gracious will is done among us]
When God breaks and hinders every evil counsel and will
which would not let us hallow God's name
nor let His kingdom come,

such as the will of the devil, the world, and our flesh;
but strengthens and preserves us steadfast
in His Word and faith unto our end.
This is His gracious and good will.

BIBLE STORY

How the Christians Prayed for the Church

Acts 4:1-31

At the time when our Lord Jesus ascended into heaven, the Christian Church was very small. The congregation in Jerusalem at that time had only about 120 members. Peter and John and the other Apostles, by the power of the Holy Ghost, preached the story of Jesus and of His resurrection from the dead. Many people believed in Jesus and became members of the Christian Church. Soon there were five thousand Christians.

But the Christians had very many powerful enemies. Especially the leaders of the Jewish people hated Jesus and His Church and tried everything in their power to destroy the Christian religion.

One day Peter and John were arrested and ordered to stop preaching about Jesus. Peter and John said: "We cannot stop. We must talk about the things that we have seen and heard."

"If you will not stop this preaching, you will be punished," the Jewish leaders said.

Peter and John went to the Christian congregation and told them all that had happened. Then the whole congregation joined in this beautiful prayer for the Church: "Lord, Thou art God, who madest heaven and earth and the sea and all things. The same powerful enemies who hated Thy holy Child Jesus and crucified Him are now threatening to destroy Thy Church. We pray Thee, give Thy servants the strength and courage to preach Thy Word. Support their preaching with miracles in Jesus' name." When they finished their prayer, they were all filled with the Holy Ghost, ready to preach about Jesus without fear.

1. **What can you say of the size of the Christian Church when Jesus ascended into heaven?**
2. **Tell how the enemies of the Church tried to destroy it.**
3. **For what did the Christian congregation pray?**
4. **How did God answer their prayer?**

BIBLE READINGS

He that hath My Word, let him speak My Word faithfully. Jer. 23:28

Let your light so shine before men that they may see your good works and glorify your Father which is in heaven. Matt. 5:16

The Kingdom of God is at hand; repent ye, and believe the Gospel. Mark 1:15

Fear not, little flock; for it is your Father's good pleasure to give you the Kingdom. Luke 12:32

God will have all men to be saved. 1 Tim. 2:4

This is the will of God, even your sanctification. 1 Thess. 4:3

BIBLE TEACHINGS

1. Jesus would have us pray mainly for spiritual gifts. Therefore, in the Lord's Prayer, we first ask God to help us keep His name holy by teaching His Word truly and by leading a holy life. We also pray God to preserve us from false teaching and an unholy life.

2. We ask our Lord to keep us in His kingdom through faith in Jesus, our Savior. We pray that He will make us eager to spread His saving Word and to lead others into the Christian Church.

3. Our heavenly Father knows what is best for us. His will is always right. We pray that He may help us to do His will cheerfully and gladly, as the angels do it in heaven. To this end God must stop the evil will of the devil, the world, and our sinful heart, and keep us faithful until death.

QUESTIONS AND ANSWERS

1. **What do we ask of our Father in the First Petition?**

   We pray, "Hallowed be Thy name."

2. **By whom is the name of God always kept holy?**

   The name of God is always kept holy by the angels in heaven.

3. **By whom should God's name likewise be hallowed?**

   By all men on earth.

4. **How is God's name hallowed?**

   In two ways: when (1) the Word of God is taught in its truth and purity, and (2) we, as the children of God, also lead a holy life according to it.

5. **When is God's Word taught in its truth and purity?**

   When nothing is added to it, nothing taken away, nor its meaning changed.

6. **What do we prove when we lead a holy life?**

   We prove that we are God's children.

7. **What will other people do when they see the good life of Christians?**

   They will praise God and honor His name.

8. **Why does the Christian earnestly pray, "This grant us, dear Father, in heaven"?**

   Without God's help the Christian cannot teach the Bible as God wants it taught, nor can he live the kind of life God wants him to live.

9. **How is God's Word profaned?**

   God's Word is profaned when something is added to it, or something taken away, or its meaning changed.

10. What happens to the name of God if we live in sin and shame?

The name of God is disgraced and dishonored among men.

11. What is the prayer of the Christian Church against false doctrine and ungodly life?

"From this preserve us, dear heavenly Father."

12. What do we ask of our Father in the Second Petition?

We pray, "Thy kingdom come."

13. What is your greatest blessing?

I have been delivered from the kingdom of Satan and have been made a member of God's Kingdom of Grace.

14. Where is God's Kingdom of Grace found?

God's Kingdom of Grace is found wherever the Gospel of Jesus Christ is preached.

15. Who are the members of the Kingdom of God?

Those who believe the Gospel are members of the Kingdom of God.

16. How has God made you a member of His kingdom?

God has brought the Gospel to me, and now I believe.

17. How does our heavenly Father enable us to believe?

Our heavenly Father gives us His Holy Spirit.

18. What precious gift do we receive from the Holy Spirit?

By His grace we receive the power to believe His holy Word.

19. Why do we need the grace of God?

By ourselves we are unable to believe the Word of our King.

20. How do we show that we are members of God's kingdom?

We lead a godly life, here in time and hereafter in eternity.

21. Why is God's kingdom called the Kingdom of Grace?

In this kingdom, God gives us only grace; that is, undeserved mercy.

22. Why do we say: "The Kingdom of God comes indeed without our prayer, of itself"?

We can do nothing to bring the Kingdom of God to ourselves.

23. Why, then, do we pray that the Kingdom of God should come?

We pray in this petition that the Kingdom of God may come to us also.

24. What should we do so that the Kingdom of God may come also to others?

We should ask God to spread His kingdom, and we should support the work of Christian missionaries with our time, talents, and treasures.

25. How long will God's Kingdom of Grace endure?

It will endure to the end of the world.

26. Which Kingdom do believers enter when they die?

When believers die, they enter the Kingdom of Glory.

27. Why do we look forward with joy to the Kingdom of Glory?

In heaven we shall see our King in all His glory and serve Him in perfect holiness forever.

28. How long will God's Kingdom of Glory endure?

God's Kingdom of Glory will endure to all eternity.

29. What do we ask of our Father in the Third Petition?

We pray, "Thy will be done on earth, as it is in heaven."

30. What is the good and gracious will of God?

His will is that all men believe in Christ and be saved.

31. How is God's will done?

The believers hallow God's name, because His kingdom has come to them.

32. How does God show His great love and mercy?

His good and gracious will is done, even when we do not pray for it.

33. Why, then, should we pray, "Thy will be done"?

So that God's good and gracious will may be done among us, and by us.

34. Whose evil counsel and will are opposed to God's will?

The counsel and will of the devil, the world, and our evil heart.

35. How do we ask God to protect us from those who would harm us?

We ask that He break and hinder their evil counsel and will, so that we might be saved.

36. How will God help us to overcome the evil counsel and will?

He will strengthen and preserve us in His Word and faith unto our end.

WORD STUDY

counsel: plan, plot
to hallow: to keep holy
militant: fighting, warlike
to profane: to treat with contempt
sanctification: holiness
seraphim: angels of high rank
triumphant: victorious

HYMN STANZAS

Our heavenly Father, hear
The prayer we offer now,
Thy name be hallowed far and near;
To Thee all nations bow.

Thy kingdom come; Thy will
On earth be done in love
As saints and seraphim fulfill
Thy holy will above.

L. H., 455:1, 2

PRAYER

Dear heavenly Father, help me keep Thy name holy. Give me Thy Spirit that I may grow in faith and lead others into Thy kingdom. Grant me grace to do Thy will, and keep me faithful to the end. Accept my prayer for Jesus' sake. Amen.

WHAT THIS MEANS TO ME

Jesus wants me to give God the first place in my life. To this end I must:

1. Read and hear His Word diligently;
2. Ask the Holy Spirit to guide me and enlighten me;
3. Do God's will cheerfully and gladly.

"Seek ye first the Kingdom of God." This shall be the chief aim in my life.

UNIT 27

THE FOURTH PETITION

Praying for Daily Bread

"Lord, Thou Openest Thine Hand"

Give us this day our daily bread.

What does this mean?

**God gives daily bread indeed without our prayer,
also to all the wicked;
but we pray in this petition
that He would lead us to know it, and to receive
our daily bread with thanksgiving.**

What is meant by daily bread?

**[Daily bread is]
Everything that belongs to the support and wants of the body,
such as food, drink, clothing, shoes,
house, home, field, cattle, money, goods,
a pious spouse, pious children, pious servants,
pious and faithful rulers, good government,
good weather, peace, health, discipline, honor,
good friends, faithful neighbors, and the like.**

BIBLE STORY

How God Fed His People in the Wilderness

Exodus 16:1-31

For many years the people of Israel were slaves in Egypt. Then God led them out of Egypt. Safely He brought them through the Red Sea and protected them from the army of Pharaoh.

When the people came into the wild and barren country east of the Red Sea, they found nothing to eat. Soon they began to cry: "Oh, if only we had stayed in Egypt, where there was plenty to eat! Here we have no food and must starve."

Then God said to Moses: "I have heard the cries of the people. I will feed them. I will let bread rain down from heaven, and everyone shall have enough to eat every day. Every morning there will be bread."

And so it was. Every morning the ground was covered with small round pieces that looked like frost. The people picked some up and said: "It is manna."

And Moses answered: "This is the bread which the Lord has given you to eat."

For forty years the people of Israel lived in the wilderness, and in all that time God never failed to send them bread from heaven.

1. Why was there no food for the people of Israel?

2. How did God give bread to the people?

3. What did the people call the bread from heaven?

4. Who gives you your daily bread?

BIBLE READINGS

The eyes of all wait upon Thee, and Thou givest them their meat in due season. Ps. 145:15

He maketh His sun to rise on the evil and on the good and sendeth rain on the just and on the unjust. Matt. 5:45

If any would not work, neither should he eat. 2 Thess. 3:10

To do good and to communicate forget not. Heb. 13:16

Give me neither poverty nor riches; feed me with food convenient for me. Prov. 30:8

Take no thought for the morrow. Matt. 6:34

Oh, give thanks unto the Lord, for He is good; for His mercy endureth forever. Ps. 106:1

BIBLE TEACHINGS

All that we have is a gift of our God. In His great love God showers His blessings upon all, upon believers and unbelievers alike.

Jesus teaches us to pray to God for our daily bread so that we may

always remember that our bread and all other goods come from God;

always thank God for His goodness and mercy;

always be willing to work honestly for our bread;

always be satisfied with what God gives us; and

always be ready to share our bread with the needy.

QUESTIONS AND ANSWERS

1. **What do we ask of our Father in the Fourth Petition?**

   We pray, "Give us this day our daily bread."

2. **How does God, as a rule, give us our daily bread?**

   He permits us to earn our daily bread by working for it.

3. **When do we come by our daily bread dishonestly?**

   When we obtain it by stealing or by fraud and falsehood.

4. **Why does God give us daily bread, even when we forget to ask for it?**

   God gives it to us, and even to the wicked, out of fatherly, divine mercy.

5. **Why, then, do we pray in this petition that God give us our daily bread?**

   We pray in this petition that He would lead us to know it and to receive our daily bread with thanksgiving.

6. **When especially should we give thanks to God for our daily bread?**

   We should especially give thanks to God for our daily bread before and after meals.

7. **What is meant by daily bread?**

   Everything that belongs to the support and wants of the body, such as home, parents, friends, good weather, and peace.

8. Why do we say "This day" and "Daily"?

We should be satisfied if each day we have enough to live on.

9. Why need we take no anxious thought for the morrow?

We are always in God's hands; He will supply our needs.

10. How do we show our gratefulness to God for the good things of life?

We recognize Him as the Giver of every good and perfect gift, and we help those who are in need.

WORD STUDY

to communicate: to share
convenient: fit, suitable, proper
flourish: blossom forth
gratefulness: thankfulness
meat: food
pious: God-fearing
poverty: being poor
spouse: husband or wife
take no thought: have no anxious thought, do not worry

HYMN STANZA

Feed Thy children, God most holy,
Comfort sinners poor and lowly;
  O Thou Bread of Life from heaven,
  Bless the food Thou here hast given!
As these gifts the body nourish,
May our souls in graces flourish
  Till with saints in heavenly splendor
  At Thy feast due thanks we render.

L. H., 659:1

PRAYER

O God, from whom all blessings flow, I thank Thee for food, clothing, and shelter. I pray Thee, protect my loved ones who are taking care of me. Bless all those who rule our country and keep peace among the nations of the earth. Give me a tender heart to share my blessings with others; through Jesus Christ, my Lord. Amen.

WHAT THIS MEANS TO ME

When I pray for "daily bread," I am asking God to give me the bodily blessings necessary for life and happiness. For these blessings I owe Him daily thanks. I must, however, be satisfied with whatever He gives me and be always willing to share my blessings with the needy.

UNIT 28

THE LAST THREE PETITIONS AND THE CONCLUSION

Praying for Deliverance

"Preserve Us, O Lord"

THE FIFTH PETITION

And forgive us our trespasses, as we forgive those who trespass against us.

What does this mean?

We pray in this petition
that our Father in heaven would not look upon our sins,
nor on their account deny our prayer;
for we are worthy of none of the things for which we pray,
neither have we deserved them;
but that He would grant them all to us by grace;
for we daily sin much and indeed deserve nothing but punishment.
So will we also heartily forgive and readily do good to those who sin against us.

THE SIXTH PETITION

And lead us not into temptation.

What does this mean?

God indeed tempts no one;

but we pray in this petition that God would guard and keep us,

so that the devil, the world, and our flesh may not deceive us

nor seduce us into misbelief, despair, and other great shame and vice;

and though we be assailed by them,

that still we may finally overcome and obtain the victory.

THE SEVENTH PETITION

But deliver us from evil.

What does this mean?

We pray in this petition, as the sum of all,

that our Father in heaven would deliver us from every evil

of body and soul, property and honor,

and finally, when our last hour has come, grant us a blessed end,

and graciously take us from this vale of tears to Himself in heaven.

THE CONCLUSION

For Thine is the kingdom and the power and the glory forever and ever. Amen.

What is meant by the word "Amen"?

That I should be certain that these petitions

are acceptable to our Father in heaven, and are heard by Him;

for He Himself has commanded us so to pray,

and has promised to hear us.

Amen, Amen, that is, Yea, yea, it shall be so.

BIBLE STORY

How God Delivered Paul from All Evils

2 Timothy 4:6-8, 17, 18

The great Apostle Paul was a prisoner in a dark jail in Rome.

Many years had passed since he had become a believer in Jesus. All that time he had dearly loved his Lord and Savior. He had traveled thousands of miles by land and sea, labored and suffered, just so he could speak to as many people as possible about Jesus and His love.

And now Paul was in chains in prison. The enemies of Jesus were not satisfied until they had Paul arrested and brought to Rome. He knew that he would never be free on earth again. In a very short time he would be put to death as a martyr for Jesus' sake.

Yet Paul was not unhappy in prison. He remembered that God had often protected him. As his mind went back over all the many evils which he had suffered in this wicked world, he remembered how God had helped him through every single one of them. He thought, for example, of how God had saved him in a shipwreck and had protected him from the poisonous snake on the island of Malta. Especially was he happy to know that God had delivered him from sin and death through the Savior Jesus Christ.

No wonder that just before his death Paul could say this joyful prayer: "The Lord shall deliver me from every evil work and will preserve me unto His heavenly kingdom; to whom be glory forever and ever. Amen."

1. What was Paul's great work?
2. Why was he put into prison?
3. Why was he happy even in prison?
4. Why was Paul ready and willing to face death?

BIBLE READINGS

God be merciful to me a sinner. Luke 18:13

When ye stand praying, forgive if ye have aught against any; that your Father also which is in heaven may forgive you your trespasses. Mark 11:25

My son, if sinners entice thee, consent thou not. Prov. 1:10

Watch and pray that ye enter not into temptation. Matt. 26:41

We must through much tribulation enter into the Kingdom of God. Acts 14:22

The Lord shall deliver me from every evil work and will preserve me unto His heavenly kingdom; to whom be glory forever and ever. Amen. 2 Tim. 4:18

BIBLE TEACHINGS

Sin is the greatest of all evils. All our troubles come from sin. Therefore Jesus teaches us to pray God to forgive us all our sins for Jesus' sake. God's forgiveness should make us so happy that we will gladly forgive those who have wronged us.

As long as we live on earth, we shall be tempted on every side to sin against God and to lose our faith. Therefore we pray God to keep us safe from every temptation and to give us strength to win the victory every time we are tempted.

Because of sin this world is full of evils. There is much suffering. The children of God, too, must suffer many sorrows and troubles. We ask God to help us through all evils and finally to deliver us forever by taking us to Himself in heaven.

QUESTIONS AND ANSWERS

1. **For what do we pray God when we say, "Forgive us our trespasses, as we forgive those who trespass against us"?**

   We pray in this petition that our Father in heaven would not look upon our sins.

2. **What would happen if God did look upon our sins?**

   He would on their account deny our prayer.

3. **Why can we not of ourselves obtain the things for which we ask?**

   We are worthy of none of the things for which we pray, neither have we deserved them.

4. **What is the plea we make to God for granting us the things for which we pray?**

   We ask that He would grant them all to us by grace.

5. **Why must we expect everything by grace?**

   We daily sin much and indeed deserve nothing but punishment.

6. **Since God, by grace, for Jesus' sake, forgives us our trespasses, how ought we to act toward those who trespass against us?**

   So will we also heartily forgive, and readily do good to, those who sin against us.

7. What do we ask of our Father in the Sixth Petition?

We pray, "And lead us not into temptation."

8. Does God ever tempt anyone to commit sin?

God indeed tempts no one, but God permits trials to come in order to test our faith and love.

9. Since God tempts no one, why then do we pray to Him, "Lead us not into temptation"?

We pray that God would guard and keep us so that the devil, the world, and our flesh may not deceive us.

10. How do temptations come?

The devil tempts us by putting wicked thoughts into our minds; the world tempts us by bad company, evil examples, promises and threats; and our flesh tempts us by evil desire.

11. What will our enemies succeed in doing if we do not watch and pray?

They will lead us off the right path and seduce us into misbelief, despair, and other great shame and vice.

12. To whom do we turn for help to resist temptation?

We turn to Jesus, the Stronger than the strong, and pray Him to stand by our side, that still we may finally overcome and obtain the victory.

13. What do we ask of our Father in the Seventh Petition?

We pray, "Deliver us from evil."

14. What leads you to believe that the last petition is the most important of all?

It is called "the sum of all."

15. Why is this petition called the sum of all?

If we are delivered from evil, we are safe and secure for time and for eternity.

16. From what evils do we ask to be delivered?

From every evil of body and soul, property and honor.

17. How does God deliver us from all afflictions?

God either takes the cross from us or He gives us strength to bear it patiently.

18. When is this prayer especially important?

When our last hour has come.

19. Why is the hour of death a serious moment?

We shall then either be completely freed from all evil or be plunged into the greatest of all evils, eternal death.

20. Who is your Savior from evil?

My Lord Jesus Christ.

21. What did Christ do to save you?

He lived and died for me and rose again.

22. What will be your earnest cry when your last hour has come?

"Lord Jesus, grant me a blessed end, and graciously take me from this vale of tears to Thyself in heaven."

23. What is the Conclusion of the Lord's Prayer?

"For Thine is the kingdom and the power and the glory forever and ever. Amen."

24. Why do we conclude the Lord's Prayer with these words of praise?

We remember that God is willing to hear our prayers and that He is able to grant us those requests which are good for us.

25. What great truth does the concluding word "Amen" set forth?

That I should be certain that these petitions are acceptable to our Father in heaven and are heard by Him.

26. Why are you sure that God will hear your prayers?

He Himself has commanded us so to pray and has promised to hear us.

27. In what word do you express your firm faith?

In the word "Amen," which means, Yea, yea, it shall be so.

WORD STUDY

to abide: to remain
affliction: misfortune, trouble
to deny: to refuse
to entice: to tempt into sin
to foil: to bring to nothing, to defeat
to seduce: to lead into wrongdoing

stay: a support
Tempter: the devil
trespasses: wrongs, sins
tribulations: great suffering and sorrow
vale: valley

HYMN STANZAS

I need Thy presence every passing hour;
What but Thy grace can foil the Tempter's power,
Who like Thyself my guide and stay can be?
Through cloud and sunshine, oh, abide with me!

I fear no foe, with Thee at hand to bless;
Ills have no weight and tears no bitterness.
Where is death's sting? Where, grave, thy victory?
I triumph still if Thou abide with me.

L. H., 552:6, 7

PRAYER

O God and Father, whose nature it is always to have mercy, forgive all my sins for Jesus' sake. Make me willing to forgive those who sin against me. Keep me safe in every temptation; and when my last hour is come, take me to Thyself in heaven, where all glory shall be Thine. Amen.

WHAT THIS MEANS TO ME

I must never place more importance on bodily blessings than on blessings of the soul. Among the spiritual blessings for which I should pray daily are:

1. Forgiveness of my sins and a forgiving heart.
2. Victory over all evil temptations.
3. Deliverance from all evils, especially those which would harm my soul.

In particular I ought to ask God to preserve me in the true faith and, when my eyes close in death, to take me to Himself in heaven.

UNIT 29

Water and the Word

"Baptized Into Thy Name Most Holy"

I. THE NATURE OF BAPTISM

What is Baptism?

Baptism is not simple water only, but it is the water comprehended in God's command and connected with God's word.

Which is that word of God?

Christ, our Lord, says in the last chapter of Matthew: Go ye and teach all nations, baptizing them in the name of the Father and of the Son and of the Holy Ghost.

II. THE BLESSINGS OF BAPTISM

What does Baptism give or profit?

It works forgiveness of sins,
delivers from death and the devil, and
gives eternal salvation to all who believe this,
as the words and promises of God declare.

Which are such words and promises of God?

Christ, our Lord, says in the last chapter of Mark:
He that believeth and is baptized shall be saved;
but he that believeth not shall be damned.

III. THE POWER OF BAPTISM

How can water do such great things?

It is not the water indeed that does them, but the
word of God which is in and with the water, and
faith, which trusts such word of God in the water.
For without the word of God the water is simple water and no Baptism.
But with the word of God it is a Baptism, that is,
a gracious water of life and a washing of regeneration
in the Holy Ghost, as St. Paul says, Titus, chapter third:
[According to His mercy He saved us] By the washing of regeneration
and renewing of the Holy Ghost,
which He shed on us abundantly through Jesus Christ, our Savior,
that, being justified by His grace,
we should be made heirs according to the hope of eternal life.
This is a faithful saying.

IV. THE SIGNIFICANCE OF BAPTIZING WITH WATER

What does such baptizing with water signify?

It signifies that the Old Adam in us should,

by daily contrition and repentance,

be drowned and die with all sins and evil lusts

and, again, a new man daily come forth and arise,

who shall live before God in righteousness and purity forever.

Where is this written?

St. Paul writes, Romans, chapter sixth:

We are buried with Christ by Baptism into death, that,

like as He was raised up from the dead by the glory of the Father,

even so we also should walk in newness of life.

BIBLE STORY

How Jesus Gave Holy Baptism to His Church

Matthew 28:16-20

Our Lord Jesus came into the world to save sinners, to make all men God's dear children. For this purpose He kept the Law of God perfectly and died on the Cross. When Jesus rose from the dead, He showed that He had really done everything that was needed to make all sinners the children of God.

All that was left to do was to tell all people what Jesus had done for them. This is the work of the followers of Jesus. When, therefore, Jesus met His disciples on a certain mountain in Galilee, He said to them: All power is given unto Me in heaven and in earth. Go ye, therefore, and teach all nations. Make all people My disciples. Do this by baptizing them in the name of the Father and of the Son and of the Holy Ghost; also by teaching them to do all things that I have commanded you.

Then Jesus made His disciples willing and eager to do their great work by giving them this wonderful promise: "Lo, I am with you alway, even unto the end of the world."

1. For what purpose did Jesus come into the world?

2. What Great Commission did Jesus give to His disciples?

3. What two things should be done to make people God's children?

4. Who baptized you?

BIBLE READINGS

Go ye, therefore, and teach all nations, baptizing them in the name of the Father and of the Son and of the Holy Ghost. Matt. 28:19

Except a man be born of water and of the Spirit, he cannot enter into the Kingdom of God. John 3:5

Ye are all the children of God by faith in Christ Jesus; for as many of you as have been baptized into Christ have put on Christ. Gal. 3:26, 27

Arise, and be baptized, and wash away thy sins. Acts 22:16

He that believeth and is baptized shall be saved. Mark 16:16

BIBLE TEACHINGS

Holy Baptism is commanded by God. Baptism is using water on someone "in the name of the Father and of the Son and of the Holy Ghost."

All people, young and old, are to be baptized; for Christ, our Lord, commanded His Church to baptize all nations. This means little children too.

By Baptism we become the children of God and have the promise of everlasting life. For Baptism washes away our sins and thus saves us from death and the devil.

(NOTE: Sponsors are to see that the children are baptized in the way Jesus commanded. They should also pray for them and help them to learn the Word of God.)

QUESTIONS AND ANSWERS

1. What is a Sacrament?

A Sacrament is a sacred act by which forgiveness of sins is imparted through the Gospel and sealed through visible elements.

2. What two Sacraments did God ordain?

God ordained Holy Baptism and the Lord's Supper.

3. What is Baptism?

Baptism is water that is used by God's command and with His promise.

4. How is Baptism usually given?

Water is sprinkled or poured on the head of the person being baptized, and the words are spoken, "I baptize thee in the name of the Father and of the Son and of the Holy Ghost."

5. Why should all people, young and old, be baptized?

All people should be baptized so that by faith in Christ Jesus they might become the children of God.

6. What has Baptism done for you?

Baptism has made me a child of God, a member of the Church, and an heir of heaven.

7. What did your sponsors promise when you were baptized?

They promised to pray for me, and to be of help, whenever necessary, in giving me a Christian education.

WORD STUDY

comprehended: contained
contrition: sorrow for wrongdoing
elements: things that are
regeneration: spiritual rebirth
to seal: to give a sign that something is true
to signify: to be a sign of, to mean
seed: children, members of a family
sponsor: a person who witnesses and answers for an infant at Baptism

HYMN STANZA

Baptized into Thy name most holy,
O Father, Son, and Holy Ghost,
I claim a place, though weak and lowly,
Among Thy seed, Thy chosen host.
Buried with Christ and dead to sin,
Thy Spirit now shall live within.

L. H., 298:1

PRAYER

I thank Thee, dear heavenly Father, that through Baptism Thou hast washed me from my sins and made me Thy child. Keep me ever mindful of all that Thou hast done for me in Holy Baptism. Let me be Thine forever, and bless me together with my dear parents and sponsors; for Jesus' sake. Amen.

WHAT THIS MEANS TO ME

I know that when I was baptized, my sins were washed away and I became a believing child of God. For this blessing I owe God a life of thankful service. I can best show my thanks by "teaching all nations" and bringing the Sacrament of Holy Baptism to them. May I never forget what God has done for me through Baptism!

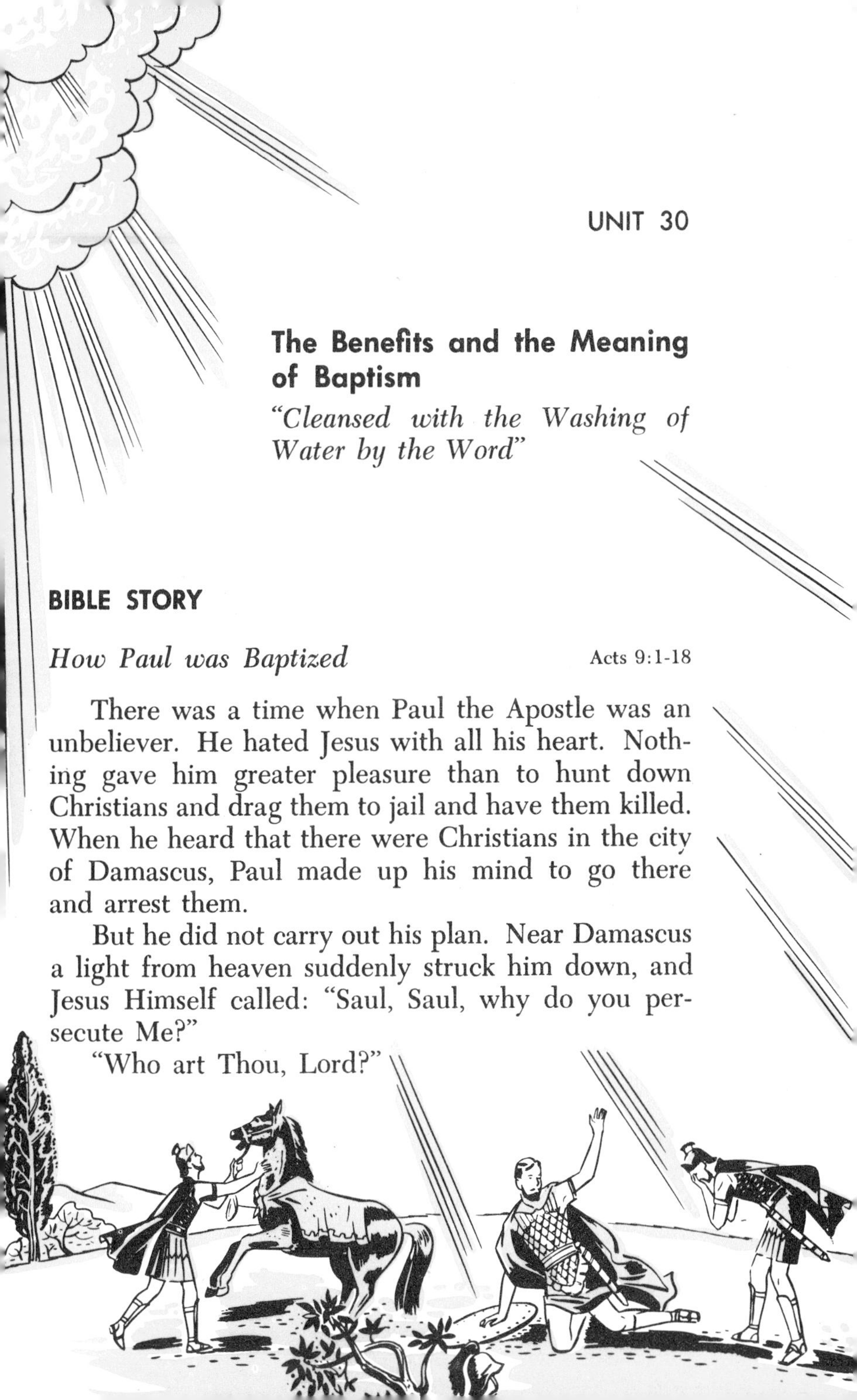

UNIT 30

The Benefits and the Meaning of Baptism

"Cleansed with the Washing of Water by the Word"

BIBLE STORY

How Paul was Baptized Acts 9:1-18

There was a time when Paul the Apostle was an unbeliever. He hated Jesus with all his heart. Nothing gave him greater pleasure than to hunt down Christians and drag them to jail and have them killed. When he heard that there were Christians in the city of Damascus, Paul made up his mind to go there and arrest them.

But he did not carry out his plan. Near Damascus a light from heaven suddenly struck him down, and Jesus Himself called: "Saul, Saul, why do you persecute Me?"

"Who art Thou, Lord?"

"I am Jesus, whom you are persecuting."

"Lord, what wilt Thou have me do?" asked Paul, trembling and astonished.

"Arise, and go into the city, and you will be told what to do."

Blind and afraid, Paul was led by his companions into Damascus. For three days he sat in his room without eating or drinking. Did he perhaps think of all his terrible sins against the Lord Jesus? If so, how sad he must have felt! Could his wicked deeds be forgiven?

On the third day a Christian of Damascus, Ananias by name, came to visit Paul. He told Paul: "The Lord Jesus, who spoke to you on the road, sent me to you. Arise, and be baptized, and wash away your sins."

Then Paul was baptized, and now he was happy and blessed. He became the greatest worker of all time in the kingdom of the Lord Jesus Christ. He is known as "the Great Apostle."

1. **Tell about the sins of Paul against Jesus.**
2. **Why did Paul stop hunting down the Christians?**
3. **How were Paul's sins washed away?**
4. **What does your Baptism mean to you?**

BIBLE READINGS

Go ye, therefore, and teach all nations, baptizing them in the name of the Father and of the Son and of the Holy Ghost. Matt. 28:19

Christ loved the Church and gave Himself for it, that He might sanctify and cleanse it with the washing of water by the word. Eph. 5:25, 26

Repent, and be baptized, every one of you, in the name of Jesus Christ, for the remission of sins.
Acts 2:38

Ye are all the children of God by faith in Christ Jesus; for as many of you as have been baptized into Christ have put on Christ. Gal. 3:26, 27

If any man be in Christ, he is a new creature.
2 Cor. 5:17

BIBLE TEACHINGS

By His holy life and by His innocent suffering and death Christ earned forgiveness of sins for us. Baptism makes this forgiveness our own. Baptism has this wonderful power because it is water used "in the name of the Father and of the Son and of the Holy Ghost."

The Holy Ghost works through Baptism and makes it a heavenly washing. By it all our sins are washed away, and we become members of God's holy family.

The great blessings of Baptism become our own through faith; for Jesus said: "He that believeth and is baptized shall be saved." This faith is given to us in Baptism by the Holy Spirit.

QUESTIONS AND ANSWERS

1. What great blessings do we receive through Baptism?
We receive forgiveness of sins, life, and salvation.

2. In what words does Jesus promise us these blessings?
He says, "He that believeth and is baptized shall be saved."

3. **How can the water of Baptism give us such great blessings?**

   It is not mere water that gives us such great blessings, but the word of God and faith.

4. **What vow did you make through your sponsors at the time of your Baptism?**

   "I renounce the devil and all his works and all his ways; I believe in God the Father, God the Son, and God the Holy Ghost; I will lead a Christian life, with the help of God."

5. **How often should you renew your baptismal vow?**

   I should renew my baptismal vow every day.

6. **Why is it not necessary to be baptized again to be made clean within?**

   God remains faithful to His promise of forgiveness given to me in Baptism.

7. **Why ought you always find comfort and joy in the fact that you have been baptized?**

   It was thus that I was born again and made a child of God.

WORD STUDY

band: a group of persons having the same purpose
to persecute: to hurt or to destroy
remission: forgiveness
to sanctify: to make holy
vow: a solemn promise
the washing of water by the word: Holy Baptism

HYMN STANZA

He that believes and is baptized
Shall see the Lord's salvation;
Baptized into the death of Christ,
He is a new creation.
Through Christ's redemption he shall stand
Among the glorious heavenly band
Of every tribe and nation.

L. H., 301:1

PRAYER

Dear Father in heaven, I thank Thee that through Baptism Thou hast forgiven all my sins and made me Thy child. Keep me in Thy favor. By Thy Holy Spirit let me live as Thy child, and give me everlasting life as Thou hast promised; through Jesus Christ, my Lord. Amen.

WHAT THIS MEANS TO ME

I must ever remember that in my Baptism I became a member of God's family. To remain God's child I must firmly continue to believe in Jesus, who earned the forgiveness I received through Baptism. My Baptism is not a magic "ticket" to heaven. Jesus reminds me of this when He says: "He that *believeth* and is baptized shall be saved."

UNIT 31

The Power to Forgive Sins

"Repent Ye, and Believe the Gospel"

THE OFFICE OF THE KEYS

What is the Office of the Keys?

It is the peculiar church power
which Christ has given to His Church on earth
to forgive the sins of penitent sinners, but
to retain the sins of the impenitent
as long as they do not repent.

Where is this written?

Thus writes the holy Evangelist John, chapter twentieth:
The Lord Jesus breathed on His disciples and saith unto them,
Receive ye the Holy Ghost.
Whosesoever sins ye remit, they are remitted unto them; and
whosesoever sins ye retain, they are retained.

THE OFFICE OF THE MINISTRY

What do you believe according to these words? (John 20:22, 23.)

I believe that,

when the called ministers of Christ deal with us

by His divine command,

especially when they exclude manifest and impenitent sinners

from the Christian congregation,

and, again,

when they absolve those who repent of their sins

and are willing to amend,

this is as valid and certain, in heaven also,

as if Christ, our dear Lord, dealt with us Himself.

CONFESSION AND ABSOLUTION

What is Confession?

Confession embraces two parts.

One is that we confess our sins;

the other, that we receive absolution, or forgiveness, from the pastor

as from God Himself,

and in no wise doubt, but firmly believe,

that by it our sins are forgiven

before God in heaven.

What sins should we confess?

Before God we should plead guilty of all sins,

even of those which we do not know,

as we do in the Lord's Prayer;

but before the pastor we should confess those sins only which we know and feel in our hearts.

Which are these?

Here consider your station according to the Ten Commandments,
whether you are a father, mother, son, daughter, master, mistress, servant;
whether you have been disobedient, unfaithful, slothful;
whether you have grieved any person by word or deed;
whether you have stolen, neglected, or wasted aught, or done other injury.

BIBLE STORY

Nathan and David

2 Samuel 12:1-13

David was a great king and a man after God's own heart. Yet he was not without sin. At one time he so far forgot God that he murdered a man named Uriah and stole his wife. For some time David was not sorry for his sins, and God was very angry with him. Finally, God sent His prophet Nathan to show David his sins.

Nathan told David this story: "There were two men living side by side, the one rich and the other poor. The rich man had very many sheep and cattle; but the poor man had nothing but one little lamb. He loved it so much that he let it drink from his own cup and eat of the family food. The little lamb was a beloved pet of the poor man and his children.

"One day the rich man had a visitor. Instead of taking a lamb from his own big flock, the rich man took the poor man's only lamb, had it killed, and served it to his guest."

King David was very angry and shouted: "As surely as there is a God, the man who did this cruel thing shall be put to death!"

Nathan answered: "You are the man! You did this when you killed Uriah and stole his wife."

Now David was truly sorry for his sins. He said: "I have sinned against the Lord."

Nathan then comforted him: "The Lord has put away your sin; you shall not die."

1. Show from the life of David that even a child of God can fall into terrible sins.

2. How did David make his sins even worse?

3. Tell how Nathan showed David the greatness of his sins.

4. In which words did David show that he was truly sorry?

5. What could Nathan then announce to David?

BIBLE READINGS

If we say that we have no sin, we deceive ourselves, and the truth is not in us.

If we confess our sins, He is faithful and just to forgive us our sins and to cleanse us from all unrighteousness. 1 John 1:8, 9

The Lord Jesus breathed on His disciples and saith unto them: Receive ye the Holy Ghost; whosesoever sins ye remit, they are remitted unto them; and whosesoever sins ye retain, they are retained.
John 20:22, 23

If I forgave anything, to whom I forgave it, for your sakes forgave I it in the person of Christ.
2 Cor. 2:10

I will give unto thee the keys of the kingdom of heaven. Matt. 16:19

BIBLE TEACHINGS

All people, even Christians, are sinners. Therefore, in almost every church service, we confess our sins and ask God for forgiveness. The pastor tells us that our sins are forgiven in the name of God. We call this the absolution.

God has given to *all* believers the power to forgive sins, and they should use it. Publicly they use this power through their pastor, whom they have called for this purpose.

Only those will have their sins forgiven who are penitent, that is, who are truly sorry for their sins and believe in Jesus as their Savior.

The power to forgive sins is also called the "Office of the Keys," because heaven is opened to a sinner when his sins are forgiven, or closed when his sins are not forgiven.

QUESTIONS AND ANSWERS

1. **How do we obtain the forgiveness which God has promised?**

   We confess our sins to God and ask Him for forgiveness.

2. **For whose sake does God forgive us the sins we confess?**

   For the sake of Jesus.

3. **Why is God willing to pardon us for Jesus' sake?**

   Jesus suffered and died for us.

4. **Where do we find this message of forgiveness?**

   We find this message of forgiveness in the Gospel.

5. **To whom has God entrusted the power to proclaim the forgiveness of sins?**

   God has entrusted it to every Christian congregation.

6. **How does the Church use this power?**

   The congregation calls a pastor to speak in its stead the absolution, or forgiveness of sins.

7. **Does the absolution spoken by the pastor hold true in heaven also?**

   Yes; it is as valid and certain, in heaven also, as if Christ, our dear Lord, dealt with us Himself.

8. **Who receives the benefit of absolution?**

   The penitent sinners.

9. **Who are penitent sinners?**

   All who are sorry for their sins and believe in Jesus as their Savior.

10. Why is the power to forgive sins called "The Office of the Keys"?

Heaven is opened to a sinner when his sins are forgiven, or closed when his sins are not forgiven.

11. Which are the words of absolution spoken by the pastor?

Upon this your confession, I, by virtue of my office as a called and ordained servant of the Word, announce the grace of God unto all of you, and in the stead and by the command of my Lord Jesus Christ I forgive you all your sins in the name of the Father and of the Son and of the Holy Ghost.

WORD STUDY

absolution: freeing from guilt of sin
contrite: sorry for wrongdoing
impenitent: not sorry for wrongdoing
manifest: clear
peculiar: special, belonging to
to purge: to make clean
to remit: to forgive, to pardon
to retain: to keep, to hold back, not to forgive
slothful: lazy
valid: true

HYMN STANZAS

With broken heart and contrite sigh,
A trembling sinner, Lord, I cry,
Thy pardoning grace is rich and free –
O God, be merciful to me!

I smite upon my troubled breast,
With deep and conscious guilt opprest:
Christ and His Cross my only plea –
O God, be merciful to me!

L. H., 323:1, 2

PRAYER

God, be merciful to me, a sinner. Purge me, and I shall be clean; wash me, and I shall be whiter than snow. Cast me not away from Thy presence, and take not Thy Holy Spirit from me. Restore unto me the joy of Thy salvation, and uphold me with Thy free Spirit. Hear me for the sake of Jesus, who loved me and gave Himself for me. Amen.

WHAT THIS MEANS TO ME

My unforgiven sins separate me from God. Therefore I ought humbly to repent and ask God's forgiveness every day. This I should do privately each day and publicly, together with my fellow believers, in the church services. If I do so, firmly believing in Jesus, who earned my forgiveness, the doors of heaven will be unlocked, and I may enter.

UNIT 32

The Nature of the Lord's Supper

"This Is My Body; This Is My Blood"

I. WHAT THE LORD'S SUPPER IS

What is the Sacrament of the Altar?

**It is the true body and blood of our Lord Jesus Christ
under the bread and wine,
for us Christians to eat and to drink,
instituted by Christ Himself.**

Where is this written?

The holy Evangelists Matthew, Mark, Luke, and St. Paul [the Apostle] write thus:

Our Lord Jesus Christ, the same night in which He was betrayed, took bread; and when He had given thanks, He brake it and gave it to His disciples, saying,

Take, eat; this is My body, which is given for you.

This do in remembrance of Me.

After the same manner also He took the cup when He had supped, and

when He had given thanks, He gave it to them, saying,

Drink ye all of it;

this cup is the new testament in My blood, which is shed for you for the remission of sins.

This do, as oft as ye drink it, in remembrance of Me.

II. THE BENEFITS OF THE LORD'S SUPPER

What is the benefit of such eating and drinking?

That is shown us by these words,

"Given and shed for you for the remission of sins";

namely, that in the Sacrament

forgiveness of sins, life, and salvation are given us through these words.

For where there is forgiveness of sins, there is also life and salvation.

III. THE POWER OF THE LORD'S SUPPER

How can bodily eating and drinking do such great things?

It is not the eating and drinking indeed that does them,

but the words here written,

"Given and shed for you for the remission of sins";

which words, besides the bodily eating and drinking,

are the chief thing in the Sacrament;

and he that believes these words has what they say and express,

namely, the forgiveness of sins.

IV. THE BENEFICIAL USE OF THE LORD'S SUPPER

Who, then, receives such Sacrament worthily?

Fasting and bodily preparation are indeed a fine outward training; but

he is truly worthy and well prepared who has faith in these words,

"Given and shed for you for the remission of sins."
But he that does not believe these words, or doubts,
is unworthy and unprepared;
for the words "for you" require all hearts to believe.

BIBLE STORY

How the Lord's Supper was First Celebrated

Mark 14:12-24

It was Thursday evening after Palm Sunday. Jesus sent Peter and John into Jerusalem to prepare the passover for Him and His twelve disciples. "Where shall we prepare it?" they asked.

Jesus said: "Go into the city, and you will meet a man carrying a pitcher of water. Follow him. He will lead you to a house. The owner of that house will let you have a large upstairs room for our meal."

When everything was ready, Jesus and the Twelve gathered around the table. Lovingly Jesus said to them: "I have had a great longing to eat this passover with you before I suffer and die."

When the meal was over, Jesus took bread; and when He had given thanks, He brake it and gave it to His disciples, saying: "Take, eat; *this is My body*, which is given for you. This do in remembrance of Me."

Then He also took the cup of wine, gave thanks,

and gave it to them, saying: "Drink ye all of it; this is the new testament in *My blood,* which is shed for you for the remission of sins. This do, as oft as ye drink it, in remembrance of Me."

1. On which day did Jesus eat the passover with His disciples?
2. Where was this meal eaten?
3. Tell what Jesus did after the regular meal.
4. What did Jesus say about the bread and the wine?

BIBLE READINGS

Take, eat; this is My body. Mark 14:22

This is My blood of the new testament, which is shed for many. Mark 14:24

The cup of blessing which we bless, is it not the communion of the blood of Christ? The bread which we break, is it not the communion of the body of Christ? 1 Cor. 10:16

As often as ye eat this bread and drink this cup, ye do show the Lord's death till He come.
1 Cor. 11:26

BIBLE TEACHINGS

The Sacrament of the Altar is also called the Lord's Supper because it was instituted by our blessed Lord on Maundy Thursday evening.

In the Holy Supper Christ gives His true body and blood to all who eat the bread and drink the wine.

We cannot understand how this can be, but we believe it because Christ said, when He gave the bread: *"This is My body"*; and when He gave the wine, He said: *"This is My blood."* What Christ says is true; furthermore, He is almighty.

QUESTIONS AND ANSWERS

1. **What Sacrament did Jesus ordain to strengthen the spiritual life begun in Baptism?**

   Jesus ordained the Sacrament of the Altar, or Holy Communion, to strengthen the spiritual life begun in Baptism.

2. **What is Holy Communion?**

   Holy Communion is the receiving of the body and blood of Christ, in, with, and under the bread and wine, for the nourishment of the soul.

3. **What earthly elements do we receive in the Sacrament of the Altar?**

   We receive bread and wine.

4. **What heavenly gifts do we receive together with the bread and the wine in the Sacrament of the Altar?**

   We receive Christ's body and blood together with the bread and the wine.

5. **Do you believe, then, that the body and blood of Christ are really present in the Sacrament?**

   Yes, I believe it.

6. **What induces you to believe this?**

   The words of Christ, "Take, eat, this is My body; drink ye all of it, this is My blood."

7. **What ought we to do when we eat His body and drink His blood, and thus receive the pledge of forgiveness?**

   We ought to remember His death, as He said, "This do in remembrance of Me."

8. Why do you wish to go to the Sacrament?

That I may learn to believe that Christ, out of great love, died for my sin; and that I may also learn of Him to love God and my neighbor.

9. What should move you to receive this Sacrament frequently?

Both the command and the promise of God as well as my need for pardon, peace, and strength.

10. How often should you receive the Lord's Supper?

Regularly and frequently, since I need food and drink for my soul.

WORD STUDY

beneficial: helpful
communion: joining together
Evangelist: one of the writers of the life and words of Christ
to fast: to go without food
to induce: to cause
to institute: to establish, to begin
naught: nothing
testament: will, agreement, promise

HYMN STANZA

We eat this bread and drink this cup,
Thy precious word believing
That Thy true body and Thy blood
Our lips are here receiving.
This word remains forever true,
And there is naught Thou canst not do;
For Thou, Lord, art almighty.

L. H., 306:4

PRAYER

We thank Thee, Lord Jesus, for Thy Holy Supper, which Thou hast prepared for Thy children on earth. Preserve unto us this blessed Sacrament until the end of days. Amen.

WHAT THIS MEANS TO ME

Jesus has told me that in the Lord's Supper I receive His true body and blood. Even though I cannot understand this mystery, yet I believe it because His Word is always true. For the strengthening of my faith in the forgiveness of sins I will celebrate this Sacrament often, as Jesus has commanded me.

UNIT 33

The Benefits of the Lord's Supper

"Him That Cometh to Me I Will in No Wise Cast Out"

BIBLE STORY

How a Father Forgave His Prodigal Son

Luke 15:11-32

A certain man had two sons. He loved them both and made their home as happy and pleasant as he could. But the younger son did not like it at home. One day he came to his father and said: "Father, give me my share of the property." The father then gave him his share.

Not long after this the younger son took all he had and left home. He went far away and wasted his goods by a wild and wicked life. As long as he had money, he had friends.

It did not take him very long to spend everything. Now all his friends were gone too. To keep himself alive, he worked in the fields, feeding pigs. He was willing to eat of the pigs' food, but he could not have even that.

Then he thought of his home. How wonderful it seemed to him now! "My father's servants have bread enough and to spare, and I must starve!" Now he saw how foolish and wicked he had been to leave home.

He made up his mind to go back to his father. After long and weary days of walking he finally came near his home.

His father had been watching for him day after day. Now, when he saw his son on the road, he ran out to meet him. With joyful heart he took his son into his arms and kissed him.

The son cried: "Father, I have sinned against God and you and no longer deserve to be called your son."

But the father would hear no more. He told his servants to bring the best clothes for his son and then make ready a big feast. He said: "This my son was dead and is alive again; he was lost and is found."

Jesus told this tender story to show how much God loves sinners and how gladly He will forgive their sins.

1. **What did the younger son ask of his father?**
2. **What did he do with his share?**
3. **What happened to him when his money was gone?**
4. **How did the father treat the son when he came home?**

BIBLE READINGS

In Christ we have redemption through His blood, the forgiveness of sins, according to the riches of His grace. Eph. 1:7

Come unto Me, all ye that labor and are heavy laden, and I will give you rest. Matt. 11:28

This is My body, which is *given for you.* Luke 22:19

This is My blood of the new testament, which is *shed for many for the remission of sins.* Matt. 26:28

Let a man examine himself, and so let him eat of that bread and drink of that cup. He that eateth and drinketh unworthily, eateth and drinketh damnation to himself, not discerning the Lord's body. 1 Cor. 11:28, 29

BIBLE TEACHINGS

With His suffering and death Christ has redeemed us and earned for us the forgiveness of all our sins. Now He graciously invites all sinners to come to Him in true faith and receive forgiveness.

In the Lord's Supper our Savior offers and gives this wonderful gift in a special way. He does this by sealing the gift with His body and His blood, to make me personally sure that my sins are forgiven.

It is therefore very important for all who go to Communion to examine themselves whether they have true faith in the promise of Jesus. For this reason children are instructed and prepared for their first Communion.

QUESTIONS AND ANSWERS

1. **What fullness of blessing does the Sacrament of the Altar impart?**

   The Sacrament of the Altar imparts forgiveness of sins, life, and salvation.

2. **Which words in the Sacrament contain the promise of this blessing?**

   The words of Jesus, "Given and shed for you for the remission of sins."

3. **What special seal does Christ affix to the words in the blessed Sacrament?**

   He affixes His body and blood as a special seal.

4. **Why can each individual communicant be sure that Jesus died for him?**

   In the Sacrament Jesus gives each person the very body and blood with which He on the Cross earned forgiveness for all.

5. **May a person who is weak in faith go to the Lord's Supper?**

   Yes, indeed; for the Lord's Supper will strengthen him in his faith.

6. **How will the Lord's Supper help us in our relationship to God?**

   The Lord's Supper will cause us to remember God's kindness and move us to be thankful.

7. How will the Lord's Supper help us in our relationship to man?

It will help us to remember that we who commune at the same altar are one in Christ, and it will help us to love and serve better all our fellow men.

8. Why should you want to receive Holy Communion frequently?

I need to have my faith strengthened, my love increased, and my soul nurtured unto life everlasting.

9. Why is it important for you to be instructed in the Christian religion before going to Holy Communion?

I should fully understand and appreciate the blessings that God intends for me in Holy Communion.

10. How should you properly prepare yourself for the right reception of the Lord's Supper?

By answering "yes" to the following questions:

a. Am I sorry that I have sinned against God?

b. Do I believe that Jesus died for my sins and gives me His body and blood in the Holy Sacrament?

c. Will I try my very best, with God's help, to lead a better Christian life?

WORD STUDY

assurance: certainty, sureness

communicant: a person who partakes of Holy Communion

to discern: to see, to recognize the importance of

to nurture: to nourish, to feed

prodigal: wasting money or other things

to seal: to make sure

HYMN STANZA

Now lettest Thou Thy guest depart
With full assurance in his heart.
For such communion, Lord, with Thee
A new life may my offering be.

L. H., 308:3

PRAYER

Dear Savior, I thank Thee that through Thy body and blood in the Holy Supper the believers are made sure of the forgiveness of their sins. Bless all who are guests at Thy Table with true faith in Thy Word and promises. Keep me faithful to the end, and give me the crown of life. Amen.

WHAT THIS MEANS TO ME

In the Lord's Supper Jesus graciously offers me the wonderful gift of forgiveness in a special way. His body and His blood, received with the bread and wine, and joined with His forgiving word, make me doubly sure that my sins are forgiven. If I celebrate the Sacrament with true sorrow over my sins and with firm faith in Jesus, who earned forgiveness for me, I will have and hold the greatest of all blessings – peace by pardon.

On his return from Worms, Luther was kidnapped by friends and taken to the Wartburg, where he remained in seclusion for almost a year.

The Life of Martin Luther

1483—1546

Martin Luther was born in the town of Eisleben, Germany, on November 10, 1483. He was the son of a hard-working miner, Hans Luther, and his wife, Margaret. Young Martin grew up in a home where the parents prayed faithfully to the saints and taught their children to do likewise. His father and mother loved their children dearly, but were also very strict with them.

LUTHER AT SCHOOL

When Martin was five years old, he went to school in Mansfeld, where his parents had moved. The subjects taught at this school were the Ten Commandments, the Creed, the Lord's Prayer, church music, together with some Latin and arithmetic. The sad part of the instruction was that Martin and his fellow pupils learned little about the *love* of God. They learned to know Jesus, not as the Friend of sinners, but as the Judge. They feared Jesus, but did not love Him.

Martin learned rapidly, for he was a bright boy and studied diligently. At the age of fourteen he was admitted to the Latin High School at Magdeburg, sixty miles from his home. Here, for the first time, Luther found a Bible. The next year his father transferred him to a school in Eisenach. Here a rich and pious young woman, Mrs. Ursula Cotta, took a special liking to him. At one time, when a group of boys was singing before her house, she invited Martin in and offered him free lodging. He readily accepted. He received free meals in another house where he taught a young child of the family. Luther was now free to devote more time to his studies. Moreover, since the Cotta family was a cultured family, Luther's stay in this home taught him to appreciate such things as music and art and helped him to develop especially his remarkable talent for music.

LUTHER AT THE UNIVERSITY

By the time Martin Luther was far enough advanced to enter the university his father had become a prosperous man. He could now afford to give Martin a college education. Recognizing the gifts of his son, the father intended that his son should become a lawyer and therefore sent him to the University of Erfurt. Here again the young student prayed and studied diligently. To increase his knowledge, Luther spent much time in the library. At the age of twenty-one he was awarded the Master of Arts degree. He now had the right to teach.

To please his father, Martin remained on at the University to read law, but he soon lost interest in that subject. More and more he studied religion and worried over his sinful condition. But no matter how hard he tried to please God, he could not find peace of soul.

LUTHER AS A MONK

One day a dear friend was torn from him by sudden death. Luther was so shaken that he became fearful and deeply disturbed. He asked himself, "What will be my lot in eternity?" A little later, while returning to Erfurt from a visit to his parents, he was overtaken by a violent thunderstorm. Almost frantic with fear, young Luther then and there determined to become a monk.

Upon his return to the University, Martin sold his books, said farewell to his friends, and, deaf to their pleadings, entered the Augustinian monastery at Erfurt. "Now," he said, "I shall certainly lead a far more God-pleasing life than I did at the University." In the "Black Cloister" Brother Martin was assigned to a small, unheated cell only seven by ten feet; the room contained a single table, chair, straw bed, and one window.

Luther continued his study of the Bible. Dressed in the black robe and little cap, to be worn day and night, he faithfully engaged in the many daily religious exercises prescribed. He also spent much time in trudging through the streets of the city, carrying a sack on his back, as was the custom then, begging for bread, butter, eggs, and whatever else he could get for the monastery. In addition, he swept the chapel, cleaned the rooms, rang the bells, and performed similar work. Back in his little cell, he diligently studied religion and philosophy and prayed to the saints, eagerly striving to earn his way to heaven through his own good works. More than ever he was searching for peace of soul; he could not find rest. One thought ever present during these days made Luther very unhappy. "I am a sinner," he said to himself, "and my sins move God to anger." As time went on, however, and as he continued to study the Bible, he made the marvelous discovery that salvation is a free gift from God through our Lord and Savior Jesus Christ, and that it is ours for the asking.

LUTHER AS PRIEST, TEACHER, AND PREACHER

In the spring of 1507, Luther, now twenty-three, was made a priest. So highly was he thought of by his superiors that he was asked to teach at the University of Erfurt and the newly founded University of Wittenberg. He soon became known as a great teacher of the Bible. Students came in great numbers to listen to his lectures.

His work as teacher was interrupted, however, by a request from his Father Superior, Dr. Staupitz, to go to Rome, where the Pope lived. He and a companion set out on foot. The journey was long and difficult; the two travelers spent their nights in monasteries along the way. When they finally saw the city before them, Luther fell on his knees and cried out, "Hail, thou holy city of Rome!" But he was greatly disappointed when he observed that the life in Rome was very sinful.

After his return five months later, Luther resumed his teaching at the University of Wittenberg. In the fall of 1512, he was honored with the title of Doctor of Divinity. Besides teaching at the University, he now also began to preach in the large Castle Church. Never before had the people heard the Word of God proclaimed so richly and so eloquently. They flocked in ever increasing numbers to hear him. In his sermons Luther warned his hearers against trying to *earn* salvation by good works and pleaded with them to accept God's offer of free salvation in Jesus.

LUTHER POSTS 95 THESES AGAINST INDULGENCES

Common in those days was the shameful practice of selling indulgences for money. People who purchased these indulgences were promised freedom from punishment on earth and in purgatory. John Tetzel, a salesman of such indulgences, came into the neighborhood of Wittenberg. He urged people

to buy forgiveness for all past, present, and future sins. Some of Luther's church members purchased these worthless indulgence letters. They boldly refused to repent of their sins. Their impenitence roused Luther to action. He refused to give such members absolution and Communion unless they showed themselves repentant. Deeply disturbed by the attitude of the people, Luther preached many sermons on repentance. Finally he wrote ninety-five theses, or sentences, in which he condemned the sale of indulgences. On October 31, 1517, he posted these Ninety-Five Theses on the University bulletin board, the door of the Castle Church. In one of his theses he stated, "Every Christian who truly repents has full forgiveness, even without letters of pardon." Thousands, both in high places and low, were glad that Luther had spoken out.

LUTHER AT WORMS

When Pope Leo X in Rome heard of the affair in Germany, he was furious and threatened Luther with excommunication if he did not recant within sixty days. But Luther remained firm, for he felt that he was right and that he had acted for the glory of God. In 1521 Luther was ordered to appear before the Diet of Worms for trial. At this convention the highest officials of the Church and of the State were present, and Luther was again asked to recant. Not one opponent could bring forward a word from the Bible to show that Luther was mistaken. Luther, therefore, refused to change anything that he had said or written.

LUTHER AT THE WARTBURG

Luther was now declared an outlaw; anyone might have killed him without fear of punishment. Although his life was in great danger, Luther was unafraid and began the return journey to Wittenberg. While he was riding through a forest, a band of masked men rushed upon him, took him prisoner, and conducted him to a castle, the Wartburg. At midnight the heavy drawbridge was lowered, and Luther disappeared behind the massive castle walls. Only a few persons knew where Luther was, and they guarded their secret well. Some people thought that Luther was dead. What they did not know was that some of his friends had secretly kidnapped him and had brought him to a safe place.

Meanwhile Luther, disguised as a knight, lived at the Wartburg. Here he translated the New Testament into the German language so that the common people might easily read and understand the Word of God. As printing with movable type had been invented shortly before this time, copies were soon in the hands of many people.

Luther remained in seclusion at the Wartburg for almost a year. Then he returned to his beloved Wittenberg and again appeared in his pulpit. He preached eight powerful sermons to clear away certain errors into which many had fallen and to show them what the new way of life was really like. He warned them against using force in their struggle against the Pope and his followers. Their sole weapon, he urged, was to be the powerful Word of God. From Wittenberg Luther went to a number of other towns and communities, everywhere counseling to use the liberty from the Papal tyranny for only one purpose – to become better Christians.

Luther lived in constant danger of being arrested and killed. But although his friends were worried, no one ever touched him. That he remained alive seems like a miracle.

LUTHER AT HOME

On June 13, 1525, Luther married Katherine von Bora, a former nun. The wedding ceremony took place in the Black Cloister in Wittenberg, now changed into a dwelling place for Luther. God blessed this marriage with three boys and three girls. Luther loved home life, and he took time to play with his children, to make music with them, and to write

letters to them when he was away from home. He was also interested in gardening and in the problems of running a household. He had many visitors. Although Luther was a man of modest means, he was very generous. His kindness and liberality to others sometimes worried his wife, especially since Luther was extremely hospitable and would freely give shelter, food, and even money to the unfortunate.

LUTHER WRITES THE CATECHISM AND HYMNBOOK

Knowing that Christian faith must be grounded in Christian knowledge, Luther organized Christian schools. To aid pastors and teachers in their instruction of children, he wrote the Small Catechism in 1529. Next to the Bible, it is the most widely used book in the Church. This book is used in schools today. Luther wrote a number of beautiful hymns, published the first Protestant hymnbook in 1524, and interested other able writers and composers in the production of good hymns and tunes. He helped in writing the Augsburg Confession, published in 1530. He completed the translation of the Old Testament in 1534. Though hampered by ill health, he was ever active, both among the people and in the quiet of his study. His writings fill many volumes. He continued to work hard until the day before he died.

LAST DAYS OF LUTHER

On January 23, 1546, at the urgent invitation of the princes of Mansfeld, Luther set out for Eisleben. Since he did not feel well enough to make the trip alone, he took his two sons Martin and Paul with him, for the weather was bad and the roads were hard to travel. Five days were required to complete the journey of eighty miles. Luther went only because this was to be a mission of loving service. He had been invited for the purpose of re-establishing peace in a family torn by bitter strife. It was a trying experience for him. After twenty days of patient counseling, however, he brought about a reconciliation. But his ailing body was now completely exhausted. In the evening of February 17 he was taken to his room to rest; near him were his sons and three close friends. Luther knew that his end was approaching. In fervent words of prayer he committed his soul to his heavenly Father. He was asked whether he was ready to die in the name of the Lord Jesus Christ, whose doctrine he had preached. He answered with a distinct "Yes." He now dropped into his last sleep, and the angels of God carried his soul into the heavenly place prepared for him and all the faithful by their Savior, the Lord Jesus Christ.

Luther died on February 18, 1546. His body was taken to Wittenberg; here a funeral service was held on February 22. Burial was made in the Castle Church, the grave being directly before the pulpit. It is still there today.

Luther is dead, but his works live after him. The Reformation of the Church, which he began, has been carried into all parts of the world. Jesus, the King of Grace, whom Luther proclaimed, lives in the hearts of millions of believers. After four hundred years Luther is still honored as the great teacher of the Lutheran Church and of all Protestantism.

"Remember them . . . who have spoken unto you the Word of God; whose faith follow, considering the end of their conversation" (Heb. 13:7).

EVA LUOMA FROM MONKMEYER PRESS PHOTO

For being near, for parents dear,
for food and drink —
I thank Thee, Lord.

Children's Prayers

MORNING

Father, we thank Thee for the night
And for the pleasant morning light;
For health and friends and loving care,
And all that makes this world so fair.
Help us to do the things we should,
To be to others kind and good;
In all we do at work or play
To grow more loving every day. Amen.

Jesus, tender Shepherd,
  Hear me while I pray;
Guide and keep me safely
  Through the coming day. Amen.

Father, lead me, day by day,
Ever in Thine own sweet way.
Show me what I ought to do;
Teach me to be kind and true. Amen.

Oh help me, Lord, this day to be
Thine own dear child and follow Thee;
And lead me, Savior, by Thy hand
Until I reach the heavenly land. Amen.

EVENING

Now I lay me down to sleep,
I pray Thee, Lord, my soul to keep;
If I should die before I wake,
I pray Thee, Lord, my soul to take;
And this I ask for Jesus' sake. Amen.

Jesus, tender Shepherd, hear me;
  Bless Thy little lamb tonight.
Through the darkness be Thou near me;
  Keep me safe till morning light. Amen.

All this day Thy hand has led me,
  And I thank Thee for Thy care.
Thou hast clothed me, warmed and fed me;
  Listen to my evening prayer. Amen.

Lord Jesus, who dost love me,
Oh, spread Thy wings above me,
  And shield me from alarm!
Though Satan would devour me,
Let angel guards sing o'er me,
  "This child of God shall meet no harm!"
Amen

Preserve us, O Lord, while waking,
And guard us while sleeping,
That awake we may be with Christ
  And in peace may take our rest. Amen.

GRACE BEFORE MEALS

Come, Lord Jesus, be our Guest;
May this food by Thee be blest.
May our souls by Thee be fed
Ever on the living bread. Amen.

God bless this food, and bless us all,
And keep us safe whate'er befall. Amen.

We thank Thee, Lord, for meat and drink,
Through Jesus Christ, our Lord. Amen.

THANKS AFTER MEALS

Many, many thanks I say
For my food and drink today.
Father, all that hungry be,
Feed them as Thou feedest me. Amen.

We thank Thee, Lord, for being near,
We thank Thee for our parents dear.
We thank Thee for the food we eat,
We thank Thee for Thy name so sweet.
Amen

GENERAL PRAYER

Jesus, help my eyes to see
All the good Thou sendest me.
Jesus, help my ears to hear
Calls for help from far and near.
Jesus, help my feet to go
In the way that Thou wilt show.
Jesus, help my hands to do
All things loving, kind, and true.
Jesus, may I helpful be,
Growing every day like Thee. Amen.

ON A BIRTHDAY

My years, dear Lord, are in Thy keeping,
My days come as a gift from Thee.
Today I ask: In Thy great mercy
Grant Thou another year to me,
That I may grow in grace and wisdom.
And let my every thought and word,
My every deed, to Thee be pleasing.
Help me to be Thine own, dear Lord;
Look down on me from heaven above
And bless me; touch me with Thy love. Amen.

ON THE WAY TO SCHOOL

I am but a little child –
Make my heart both pure and mild;
Thus a temple it shall be,
Dedicated, Lord, to Thee. Amen.

Holy Jesus, every day
Keep me in the narrow way;
And when earthly things are past,
Bring my ransomed soul at last
Where it needs no star to guide,
Where no clouds Thy glory hide. Amen.

FOR PARENTS AND LOVED ONES

Hold them closely in Thy keeping,
  All the dear ones that I love;
Keep them safe, awake or sleeping,
  Lord of earth and heaven above!
Guard them, oh, most tenderly;
They are safe, if kept by Thee. Amen.

WHEN SICK

Tender Jesus, meek and mild,
Look on me a little child.
Help me, if it be Thy will,
To recover from all ill.

AT PLAY

Help me, Lord, to be today
Very kind in all my play;
Make me helpful, make me strong,
Show me what is right and wrong. Amen.

Jesus, Friend of little children,
    Be a Friend to me;
Take my hand, and ever keep me
    Always close to Thee. Amen.

PRAYER OF THANKSGIVING

Lord, bestow a grateful heart,
For the gifts Thou dost impart
To a little child like me
Who depends alone on Thee. Amen.

Books of the Bible

The Bible is divided into two parts, the Old Testament and the New Testament. There are sixty-six books in the Bible: thirty-nine in the Old Testament and twenty-seven in the New Testament.

BOOKS OF THE OLD TESTAMENT

Historical Books

Gen'e-sis
Ex'o-dus
Le-vit'i-cus
Num'bers
Deu-ter-on'o-my

The Pen'ta-teuch (Five Books of Moses)

Josh'u-a
Judg'es
Ruth
First Sam'u-el
Second Sam'u-el
First Kings
Second Kings
First Chron'i-cles
Second Chron'i-cles
Ez'ra
Ne-he-mi'ah
Es'ther

Poetical Books

Job
Psalms
Prov'erbs
Ec-cle-si-as'tes
or The Preacher
Song of Sol'o-mon

Prophetical Books

Major Prophets

I-sa'iah
Jer-e-mi'ah
Lam-en-ta'tions
E-ze'kiel
Dan'iel

Minor Prophets

Ho-se'a
Jo'el
A'mos
O-ba-di'ah
Jo'nah
Mi'cah
Na'hum
Hab-ak'kuk
Zeph-a-ni'ah
Hag'gai
Zech-a-ri'ah
Mal'a-chi

BOOKS OF THE NEW TESTAMENT

Historical Books

Mat′thew
Mark
Luke
John
The Acts of the Apostles

Epistles

Ro′mans
First Co-rin′thi-ans
Second Co-rin′thi-ans
Ga-la′tians
E-phe′sians
Phi-lip′pi-ans
Co-los′sians
First Thes-sa-lo′nians
Second Thes-sa-lo′nians
First Tim′o-thy
Second Tim′o-thy
Ti′tus
Phi-le′mon
He′brews
James
First Pe′ter
Second Pe′ter
First John
Second John
Third John
Jude

Prophetical Book

The Revelation of St. John

Alternate Bible Stories

UNIT A

God, the Creator of All Things	Gen. 1:1-31
God Loves Even His Fallen Creatures	Gen. 3:15
God Knows All About Me	Ps. 139:1-10
God Loves Me and Takes Care of Me	Psalm 103

UNIT B

One Lord	Deut. 6:4
The Oneness of God	John 17:21, 22
The Thrice-Holy God	Is. 6:1-4
The Lord — the Lord — the Lord	Num. 6:24-26
Jesus Promises the Comforter	John 14:15-18

UNIT C

Jesus, the Bible Student	Luke 2:42-47
The Seed Is the Word of God	Luke 8:4-18
Four Kinds of Heart Soil	Matt. 13:1-23
The Prophets Tell of Jesus	Acts 10:43
The Whole Bible Is the Jesus Book	Luke 24:25-27
The One Thing Needful	Luke 10:38-42

UNIT ONE

The Law Came from God	Ex. 20:1-17
The Children of Israel Worship a Golden Calf	Ex. 32:1-6
Faith and a Slingshot	1 Sam. 17:23-54
Gods Who Cannot Hear or See	Psalm 115
The Prophets of a False God Destroyed	1 Kings 18:17-40

UNIT TWO

First He Cursed; Then He Cried	Matt. 26:69-75
Abraham Put His Servant Under Oath	Gen. 24:3
The Men Who Swore to Kill	Acts 23:12
Ancient Witchcraft	Deut. 18:10-12
Woe to the Make-Believe Church Members!	Matt. 23:13-28
Hannah Asked and Thanked God for a Baby Boy	1 Samuel 1 and 2
A Blind Man Glorified God for Receiving His Sight	Luke 18:43

UNIT THREE

King Saul Refused to Listen to God's Word	1 Sam. 15:10-23
Mary Listened to God's Word	Luke 10:38-42
A Captain Wished to Hear the Gospel	Acts 10:33
The Early Christians Worshiped Regularly	Acts 2:42
Sunday Preferred	Acts 20:7
None Too Poor to Support the Church	Mark 12:41-44

UNIT FOUR

Jesus Is Obedient to His Parents	Luke 2:51
A Great King Honors His Mother	1 Kings 2:19
A Wicked Son Grieves His Father	2 Sam. 15:1-14
Bad Boys Ridicule a Preacher	2 Kings 2:23, 24
The Model Son Provides for His Heartbroken Mother	John 19:25-27

UNIT FIVE

Cain Kills His Brother Abel	Gen. 4:8
Paul Watches the Stoning of Stephen	Acts 7:58, 59
Remorse and Suicide	Matt. 27:3-5
Hate and Jealousy in a Home	Gen. 37:3-11
A Master Gets Help for His Servant	Matt. 8:5-13

UNIT SIX

The First Wedding	Gen. 2:18-24
Rebekah Becomes Engaged	Gen. 24:49-59
David Takes Another Man's Wife	2 Sam. 11:2-4
A Supper Party Watches an Unclean Show	Mark 6:21-28

UNIT SEVEN

A Traveler to Jericho Beaten and Robbed	Luke 10:25-37
A Disciple Becomes a Thief	John 12:1-9
Gehazi's Tricks and Lies	2 Kings 5:20-24
Abraham Helps and Befriends His Nephew	Gen. 13:1-12
Zacchaeus Makes Good	Luke 19:8
The More You Give, the More You Have	Mal. 3:8-10

UNIT EIGHT

False Witnesses Arose Against Jesus	Matt. 26:59-61
Lies at a Court Trial	1 Kings 21:5-14
Willing to Betray for Money	Matt. 26:14-16
Jonathan Defends His Friend	1 Sam. 19:4
The People of Capernaum Spoke Well of the Centurion	Luke 7:4, 5
The Tongue — a Power for Good or for Evil	James 3:5-10

UNIT NINE

Absalom Covets a Crown	2 Sam. 15:1-6
Covetousness Is Foolish	Luke 12:15-21
Paul Did Not Covet Another Man's Servant	Philemon
The Contented Heart	Heb. 13:5, 6

UNIT TEN

The Jealous God Punishes Evildoers	Genesis 7
Two Cities Experienced the Wrath of God	Genesis 19
The Mills of God Grind Slowly	Luke 19:41-44
Grace and Every Blessing to Him Who Obeys	Gen. 22:15-18

UNIT ELEVEN

The Law of the Lord Is Good	Ps. 19:7-14
The Law Is Written in the Heart	Rom. 2:14, 15
The Law Serves as a Curb	1 Tim. 1:8-10
The Law Serves as a Mirror	Matt. 5:21, 22

UNIT TWELVE

What the Skies Tell Us	Ps. 19:1-6
I Only Am God	Is. 45:5-7
The Man Who Said, "I Believe."	Mark 9:23, 24
The Mother Who Would Not Take "No" for an Answer	Matt. 15:21-28

UNIT THIRTEEN

One Angel Against 185,000 Men. Who Won?	2 Kings 19:20-36
Angels Glorify the Birth of Christ	Luke 2:13, 14
An Angel Rescues Peter from Prison	Acts 12:1-17
An Angel Carries a Saved Soul into Heaven	Luke 16:19-22
Satan, Prince of Evil Angels, Defeated by Jesus	Matt. 4:1-11
When Angels Will Appear in the Skies	Matt. 25:31-46

UNIT FOURTEEN

Paradise Lost	Genesis 3
Fearfully and Wonderfully Made	Ps. 139:14
God Hath Made of One Blood All Nations	Acts 17:24-26
The Normal Span of Life	Ps. 90:1-12
Paradise Regained	Rev. 7:9-17

UNIT FIFTEEN

God Preserved Noah's Family Alive	Gen. 9:1-3
God Provided Bread from Heaven	Ex. 16:11-15
Ravens Deliver Bread	1 Kings 17:1-8
Lot Is Saved from the Burning Cities	Genesis 19
Enough Flour in the Barrel	1 Kings 17:8-16
Sustained by the Power of God	Is. 40:28-31

UNIT SIXTEEN

A Savior for the Lost	Luke 19:1-10
Good News for a Bad Woman	John 4:25, 26
Safe in the Hollow of God's Hand	John 10:27-39
Mighty to Save	Matt. 8:23-27
A Little Girl Saved from Death	Mark 5:35-43
Our Redeemer — Divine, Yet Human	Matt. 4:2

UNIT SEVENTEEN

To Fulfill All Righteousness	Matt. 3:13-15
To Do His Father's Will	Matt. 26:36-46
The Son of God Condemned to Death	Matt. 26:57-68
He Died for All	Matt. 27:46-50

UNIT EIGHTEEN

Along the Way of Sorrows	Luke 23:27-33
On Golgotha	John 19:17-34
The Burial of Jesus	John 19:38-42
Bought and Paid For	1 Peter 1:18, 19
Redeemed that I Might Serve	1 Cor. 6:19, 20

UNIT NINETEEN

Jesus Lives	Matt. 28:1-5
Sorrow Changed into Rejoicing	Mark 16:1-15
It Took Them by Surprise	Luke 24:13-35
Jesus at the Right Hand of the Father	Mark 16:19, 20

UNIT TWENTY

Stephen Looks into Heaven	Acts 7:55, 56
A Glimpse into Heaven	Rev. 7:9-17
King of Kings	1 Peter 3:18-22
The Lamb Worthy of Great Honor	Rev. 5:1-10

UNIT TWENTY-ONE

In the Form of a Dove	Luke 3:21-23
Stephen Is Filled with the Holy Ghost	Acts 7:55-60
A Jesus Hater Turned into a Jesus Lover	Acts 9:1-20
A Man from Africa Receives the Holy Ghost	Acts 8:26-39

UNIT TWENTY-TWO

The Net Filled with Every Kind of Fish	Matt. 13:47-50
A Large Congregation	Acts 2:41-47
You Cannot Fool God	Acts 5:1-11
The Man Without a Wedding Garment	Rev. 3:7-13
A Loyal Church	Matt. 22:11-14

UNIT TWENTY-THREE

The Father Who Took Back His Runaway Son	Luke 15:11-24
A Penitent Sinner Who Went Home Justified	Luke 18:9-14
Christians Must Forgive Each Other	Matt. 18:21-35
The Church Has Power to Forgive Sins	Matt. 18:18-20

UNIT TWENTY-FOUR

Death Is a Sleep	Mark 5:38-43
The Resurrection Body	1 Cor. 15:51-57
The Last Judgment	Matt. 25:31-46
Christ Promises Eternal Life	John 10:27-30

UNIT TWENTY-FIVE

Grace Before Meat	John 6:1-15
Mary Petitions Jesus for a Miracle	John 2:1-11
The Centurion Presents His Request	Matt. 8:1-13
Kyrie, Eleison! (Lord, have mercy!)	Matt. 15:21-28
A Prayer of Intercession	Luke 23:32-34

UNIT TWENTY-SIX

Our Savior's Great Prayer for the Church	John 17
Jesus Prays for Peter	Luke 22:31-34
God Hears Elijah's Prayer	1 Kings 18:17-39
Beware of False Prophets	Matt. 7:15-23

UNIT TWENTY-SEVEN

Food from the Deep	Luke 5:1-7
Food for 5,000	John 6:1-14
Consider the Lilies	Matt. 6:19-34
The Farmer Who Forgot About God	Luke 12:13-21
Diligence and Thrift Bring Blessings	Prov. 31:10-31

UNIT TWENTY-EIGHT

How Often Must We Forgive Our Brother?	Matt. 18:21, 22
The Man Who Was Ready to Forgive	Gen. 50:15-21
The Devil Tempted Christ	Matt. 4:1-11
Bad Company Brings Bad Temptations	Luke 22:54-62
The Lions Could Not Harm Him	Dan. 6:10-23
Delivered from All Evil	Luke 16:19-22

UNIT TWENTY-NINE

John Baptizes Jesus in the Jordan	Mark 1:9-11
Jesus Blesses Little Children	Mark 10:13-16
A Jailer and His Household Are Baptized	Acts 16:25-33
The Ethiopian Receives Baptism	Acts 8:26-39

UNIT THIRTY

Christ's Command to Baptize	Mark 16:14-16
Baptism Doth Also Now Save Us	1 Peter 3:18-22
The Pharisees and Lawyers Refused to Be Baptized	Luke 7:30
3,000 Baptized on One Day	Acts 2:41-43

UNIT THIRTY-ONE

Whosesoever Sins Ye Remit	John 20:19-23
The Prodigal Son Is Forgiven	Luke 15:11-23
Tears of Penitence	Matt. 26:69-75
A Prayer of Penitence	Psalm 51
Winning the Erring Brother	Matt. 18:15-20

UNIT THIRTY-TWO

Celebrating the Passover	Mark 14:12-26
Holy Communion Instituted	Luke 22:14-20
The Real Presence	1 Cor. 10:16
"All One Body We"	1 Cor. 10:17

UNIT THIRTY-THREE

Be Not as the Hypocrites	Matt. 6:16-18
Thy Righteousness — My Glorious Dress	Matt. 22:11-14
Hold Fast Thy Crown	Rev. 3:10-13
Power to Overcome the World	1 John 5:1-5